HADRIAN'S WALL IN 1801

HADRIAN'S WALL IN 1801

Observations on the Roman Wall

by

REV. JOHN SKINNER F.S.A.

Edited by

HOWARD and PETER COOMBS

KINGSMEAD PRESS

First Published 1978
© Howard & Peter Coombs

SBN 901571 93 8

Kingsmead Press
Rosewell House
Kingsmead Square
Bath

Text set in 11/13 pt VIP Bembo, printed by photolithography,
and bound in Great Britain at The Pitman Press, Bath

PREFACE

In 1970, when we were preparing material for the publication of "The Journal of a Somerset Rector" we were shewn in addition to the water-colour paintings by John Skinner, which we used in that publication, a M/S journal dated 1801 of a journey made to Hadrian's Wall. This proved to be an interesting diary of his walk along the course of the Wall from 11th – 26th September, neatly illustrated with drawings not only of places of interest along the route but also of many Roman inscriptions found.

We are indebted to the Rev. R. E. S. Bennett, the rector of Camerton for the loan of this note-book, which we understand will eventually be deposited in the County Museum at Taunton, together with the other Skinner manuscripts and drawings in his possession.

The following notes may be of interest to those wishing to compare this, the original note-book with the transcript in the British Museum (presumably copied by his brother Russell) from which Mr. K. S. Painter produced the version printed in the B. M. Quarterly volume 37(1973). This latter is clearly an edited transcription with the illustrations redrawn, in almost every case losing something in the process.

September 5th	. . . One page of the Journal crossed out. This is followed by two pages of drawings and one water-colour. Three pages have here been cut out.
September 6th	There is no record under this date. (The B.M. transcription contains a short note.)
September 10th	Following this date one page is cut out, then one page quoting Camden.
September 14th	The three coins mentioned are illustrated.
September 23rd	No record either in this or the B.M. transcription.
September 25th	This date is given twice! . . . headed Carlisle, and the next day . . . Bowness.
September 29th	The B.M. date is probably wrong and should be part of the 28th entry as per original note book. This alters all subsequent dates, i.e. Journal . . . Sept. 29th; B.M. Oct. 1st; the probable date is Sept. 30th. We have retained the dates given throughout this original note book.

INTRODUCTION

John Skinner was inducted into the living of St. Peter's, Camerton on Sept. 13th, 1800, but although he moved into the Parsonage in November of that year. . . . "Manningham, my brother-in-law coming to Bath in the spring (of 1801) with a friend of his named Muller, spent some days at the Parsonage, and persuaded me to join them at Sidmouth. I did not feel disposed to do so at first, but an event afterwards occurred which decided me, that was the loss Mr. James, rector of Radstock, sustained in his Parsonage – that having been burnt to the ground by accident. I therefore relinquished mine to him for a year while he was building, but Mr James's new house not being fit to receive him I did not get back to Camerton until Lady Day 1802!" We now know where he spent part of that year away from his parish, – at the Lakes, on the Wall and in Anglesey.

Readers interested in the character and temperament of this extraordinary diarist will note that as early as 1801 he shewed unmistakable signs of persecution mania, of depressive tendencies and of the unbalance which led to his tragic end thirty-eight years later. . . .

"At Haddon on the Wall, where I stopped to enquire the distance, I was insulted by a drunken fellow who declared I was a spy; of course I took no notice of him and left him drinking in the Ale-house. However, half an hour after he overtook me on the road and behaved in such a manner that I really thought I would have come to close quarters, but at length he passed on full gallop. Whether this man had prejudiced the people against me, or whether they might not of themselves give in to this man's ideas I am yet to learn, but on my arrival at the Inn at Harley at 10 o'clock they received me in such a curious manner that my feelings overcame my interests and I left the house." Poor Skinner! this could happen to anybody, but it is not coincidence that such treatment happens to him more often than to others.

Again – ". . . but I must remark by the way that civility to strangers by no means appears to be a characteristic of the people of Northumberland more than in Wales. At one cottage I passed this morning close to the Wall, I saw a woman at her door with a sheep-dog by her side and as I approached nearer, she shut herself in the house and endeavoured to set the dog on me; had I not been armed with a stick, in all probability I might have been bitten. At Chesters I have just been speaking of it was not much better, for the farmer who was in the field with his reapers did not attempt to call off his dog when he was running to me, and it was some time before I could persuade him that my intentions were pacific in visiting these parts. How absurd is the idea of Arcadian simplicity and benevolence in the lower orders. Whenever I have made any observations I am sure it has been quite the reverse, and the more uninformed the people, the more brutal and selfish I have always found them."

And later . . . "but I do not wish to become misanthropic; tourists think highly of the kindness and simplicity of the inhabitants of this country as they do of the Welsh, but alas! I did not experience it, and yet it is not difficult to please me where only the intention is good."

There are many examples in the Journals already published of his self-examination; he knew his faults, but when he says he must not become misanthropic he is too late, mistrust of his fellow humans is built into his character.

JOURNAL OF A SOMERSET RECTOR
1801

Wednesday August 19th, LONDON
Went on board a Newcastle trader this day at 8 o'clock as the wind was to the east and we were obliged to warp out, but the Pool being crowded with ships, we soon came aground where we lay till the evening. Nothing can more fully testify the riches and commercial prosperity of this country than a view of the river from London Bridge to Greenwich. Thousands of merchant ships of all nations are ranged in lines on each side of the shore, some receiving, some discharging their freights. Innumerable boats of various types and descriptions passing to and fro give animation to the scene and keep alive that attention. My mind was so much interested with these various objects that I had no occasion to regret being detained on the first stage of my voyage, for where could I find more diversity, or a more ample field for observation than at this place? It is not the charms of nature alone that should interest the eye of the traveller. Works of industry and art, where the powers of the human mind are exhibited, are no less worthy of his notice, and the busy scenes of commercial enterprise form no unpleasing contrast to the serene tranquillity of a remote and uncultivated country.

August 20th
We were only able to proceed a small distance further down the river, and came to anchor opposite Greenland Docks. On going ashore, I had an opportunity of observing the manner in which they boil the whale's blubber which is brought home in casks. This is done in large square cisterns or coppers near the spot where this stinking commodity is landed. I was content with a casual glance at the process, for neither my eyes nor my olfactory nerves were much gratified in the observation. Some ships, if they have been fortunate, will bring home from 100–150 tons of blubber which may be worth from £20–30 a ton, which independent of the whalebone, must return a fine profit to the shipowners. So indeed it ought, considering the expense, risque and danger they undergo in this precarious fishery.

August 21st
This day we floated down as far as Gravesend and I went on shore for an hour to read the papers. The wind still contrary.

August 22nd
Proceeded as far as the Hope where we anchored.

August 23rd

Arrived at the Nore and came to an anchor off Southend on the Essex side of the river. This of late years has become a bathing place where many resort in preference to Ramsgate and Margate, but I cannot think the water so clean or so salt. We got underweigh again before the evening, and the wind coming more to the South West we were able to continue under sail all night.

August 24th

This morning, had a distinct view of Harwich and the Guard Fort. The town of Orford with its castle, has a good appearance. This coast is, generally speaking flat, and the navigation difficult on account of the many sand-banks stretching along the shore. Aldborough another borough-town is situated on the coast about four or five miles from Orford, . . . apparently of the same size. Beyond it again is Southwold which we passed in the night.

August 25th

This morning getting up at five o'clock, I found we were opposite to Lowestoft, another town on the Suffolk coast supposed to be the most easterly point of the

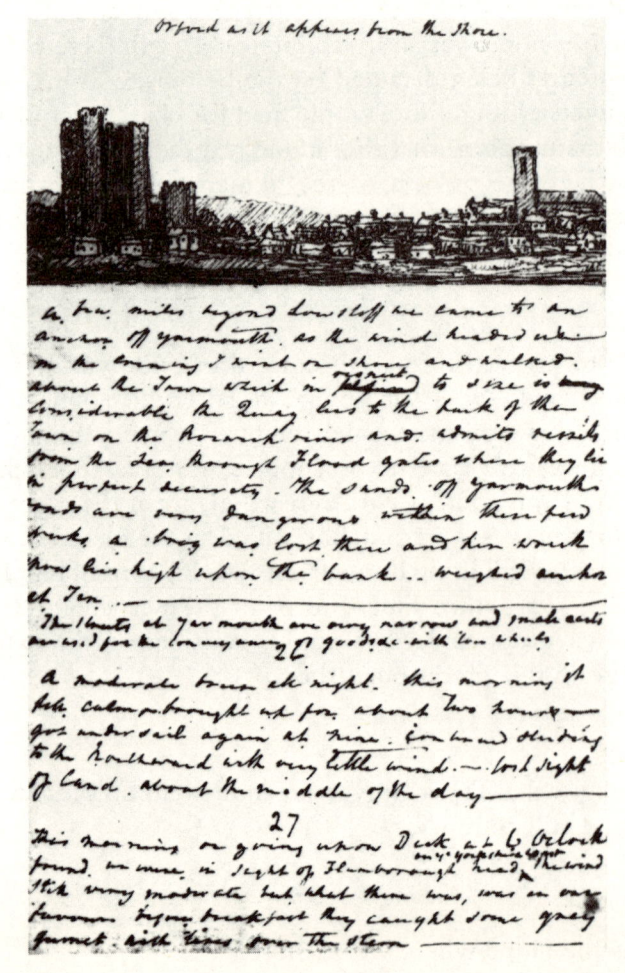

Kingdom. This place carries on a great fishery in herrings and has lately become a bathing-place. It is built on an eminence, and the gardens of the houses incline on a steep descent towards the sea. There appears to be some fine sand and some good building, so that it is well calculated for company. I counted five bathing-machines on the shore. I did a drawing of Orford as it appeared from the shore. A few miles beyond Lowestoft, we came to anchor off Yarmouth. As the wind headed us in the evening, I went on shore and walked about the town which in respect to size, is considerable. The quay lies to the back of the town on the Norwich River and admits vessels from the sea through flood-gates where they lie in perfect security. The sands off Yarmouth Roads are very dangerous; within these few weeks a brig was lost there, and her wreck lies high upon the bank. Weighed anchor at ten. The streets at Yarmouth are very narrow, and carts are used for the conveyance of goods, – with low wheels.

August 26th
A moderate breeze all night; this morning it fell calm and brought up for about two hours. Got under sail again at nine and continued standing to the northward with very little wind. Lost sight of land about the middle of the day.

August 27th
This morning, on going up on deck at six o'clock found on course in sight of Flamborough Head on the Yorkshire coast, the wind still very moderate, but what there was, was in our favour. Before breakfast they caught some grey gurnet with lines over the stern. Towards evening, came opposite to Scarborough, but the weather being rather hazy could not see the town distinctly. The ruins of a castle appeared on a high cliff jutting out into the sea. The position is very strong by nature; very high and dangerous cliffs along this coast. Passed Robin Hood's Bay, and just as night was closing in were abreast of Whitby. A brisk wind continued to favour us the whole night.

August 28th . . . SHIELDS
At half past five this morning, a pilot came on board from Shields as soon as I was up, and I was not a little pleased to see the place of my destination so near at hand, however it was nearly eight before I got on shore. On entering the harbour, the ruins of the Castle are seen to great advantage to the right. Like the building at Scarborough, it stands on a rocky cliff; the outer walls are extensive but as I mean to observe this place more particularly I shall delay my account of it until the evening. This ruin is at the mouth of the Tyne, and near it of late years many houses have been built for company who resort here as a bathing-place. From hence to Shields I walked nearly a mile on a high bank rising eighty or a hundred feet above the river. The greater part of the town of North Shields is on a level with the water below. The houses are irregular and are confined, the streets being only sufficiently wide to admit a cart, and miserably dirty. All manner of nastiness obstructing the passage, but what more disgusted me was the butchers' shops where lambs were killing before the door. A sight of this kind I should always wish to avoid, but where the street is only fourteen or fifteen feet wide it cannot be done easily. Were it not for its vicinity to the river which must carry off a great deal

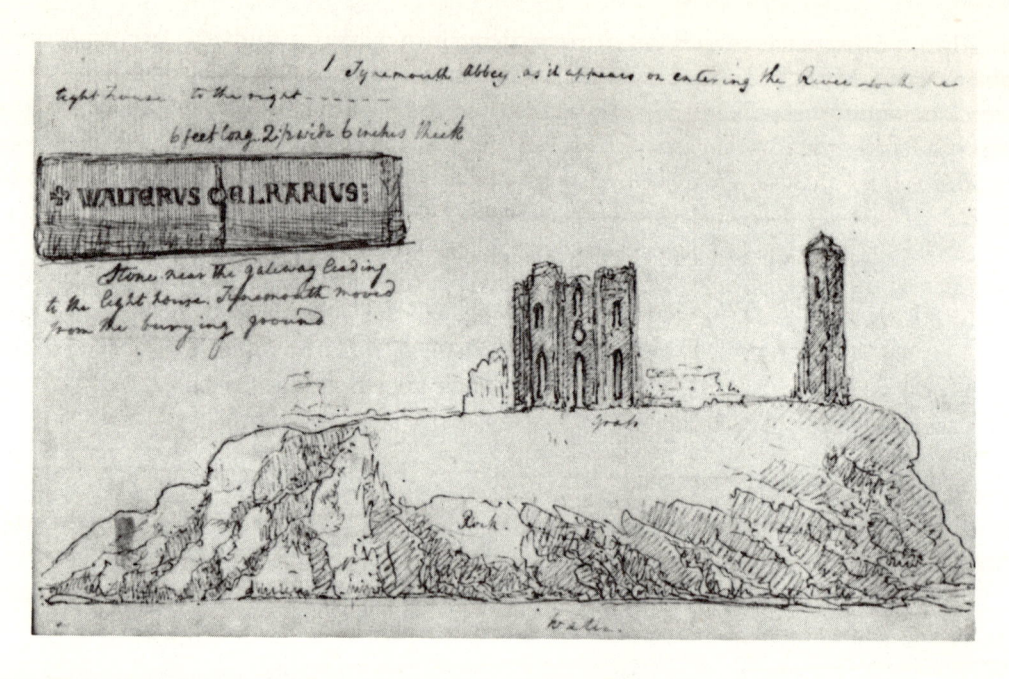

of its filth, this place would certainly be very unwholesome. The view of the sea and the river is very striking from the higher ground, and the vast number of vessels on both sides of the water afford a striking picture of the commerce of these parts. I forgot to observe that South Shields is on the opposite side of the water which is here about a quarter of a mile in width.

After breakfast at the Half Moon Inn, I returned to Tynemouth to take a nearer view of the ruin which had before engaged my attention. The approach is through a strong gateway which has not long since been considerably enlarged and is now used as barracks. From this gateway a wall extends along the cliff facing the south, the rocks being very steep on this side must have rendered it secure from attack. Another wall runs to the north and encloses altogether an area of about six acres, encompassing nearly the whole of the Peninsula. On this site, is built a lighthouse and a dwelling house by a Mr. Villars, which modern erections have not a little contributed to the dilapidation of the ancient edifice. Although this place was strongly fortified both by nature and by art towards the outward approach, it is evident from what remains of the interior that is was formerly the seat of the arts rather than of arms. From the account I have just read, I find it was a Priory of very great antiquity as St. Herebold companion to St. John of Beverly was monk and abbot here in the beginning of the 8th century. Previous to this, Edwin King of Northumberland who died in 633, built a chapel of wood at Tynemouth wherein his daughter took the veil. In all probability the Romans had first chosen this spot as a camp, for not many years ago an altar was dug up here, dedicated to Jupiter, and Agricola is said to have extended his chain of forts from this point. But leaving these very remote researches, what remains of the present building shows it was formed in the finished style of Gothic architecture brought into England after the Conquest. The east-end which I have taken a sketch of, is exceedingly light and beautiful and resembles very much the entrance to Vale Crucis Abbey in the Vale

East End of Tynemouth Abbey - near view -

of Llangollen, North Wales. The windows are nearly twenty feet high, richly ornamented with moulding and carved work. The little edifice adjoining, I suppose to have contained a tomb and shrine of St. Oswin, is most highly finished and is still in good preservation. It is about twenty feet long and half as much in breadth and height. On this south side is an entrance from without with two windows to the right hand; on the north there were three windows but now stopped up. To the east was an aperture which I have given in the drawing, beneath this probably stood an altar. On each side are two niches for statues and places for Holy water etc. The side walls are ornamented with pilasters from whence spring the groins and arches of stone for the support of the roof which is formed of thin brick. The joins of the arches are enriched with sculptures representing the Apostles in half lengths; round each figure are raised letters in old English characters imploring the intercession of the divine personages such as . . . SANCTIS PETRIUS ORA PRO NOBIS varying the name of the person to whom it is inscribed. There are also effigies of Our Saviour at the Day of Judgement over which is this inscription "IN DIE JUDICII LIBERARE NOS". On the outside of the

11

building are the two coats of arms supported by cherubs, the one charged with a cross, the arms of the monastery of St. Albans on which this was dependent, the other with three crowns, the arms of Tynemouth monastery.

A great part of the ground surrounding the ruin is used as a burying place, for the Parish Church stands some distance from the town. Malcolm King of Scots, and Edward his son slain near Alnwick in 1094 were buried here; nothing is to be seen of their monument. Below this Abbey underneath the rocks are some small wooden boxes for the purpose of bathing; they are by no means so commodious as those which are on wheels, and the bathers are obliged to walk some way before they come to the water. Across the mouth of the harbour runs a bank of sand which at low water will not admit vessels of any draught, but there are very skilful pilots who take charge of the ships at a stated price, I believe 15 pence a foot according to the water they draw.

Besides the coal trade which employs some hundreds of craft of various descriptions, a good deal of commerce is carried on from hence with Russia and the East Countries in hemp, iron, tallow, timber, grain, etc; they have also five sail for the Greenland fishery, one of them is now lying opposite the Inn window. She mounts eighteen guns, and is of large dimensions; this year she has caught fifteen whales.

Some of the ships employed in the coal trade are also very large, that is, from three to four hundred tons, but they compute their measurements here by keels which are lighters, each carrying eight pit chaldrons or sixteen London. Some of the largest colliers will carry twenty-five keels or four hundred London chaldrons; these are bought on the spot for about nine shillings each and sold in the Metropolis at above triple the sum, but when one considers the pay of the sailors who receive each five guineas, sometimes ten, the voyage, victualling the vessels, the wear of the cordage, the expenses attending loading and unloading and various other outgoings, their profits are not so considerable as they appear at first sight. The vessels after having discharged their freight in the Thames, are obliged to take on ballast of dirt, mud, and sand which the boats belonging to Trinity House clear out of the shoal places on the river. For this they pay a stated price. On their return to Shields, this rubbish is discharged on each side of the Tyne, and has so much accumulated in the course of years, that large hills are formed nearly a hundred feet high and of great extent, towering above the houses. If there is so much collected of this useless mass to which each returning vessel perhaps contributes only a fourth part of her tonnage, what must have been the quantity of coal carried from hence. If all was heaped up from the time they first began the trade! Snowdon would appear a wart to it. The coal pits run to about a hundred fathoms in depth and veins from three to six feet in thickness. The pitmen are much annoyed by vapours and foul air which frequently occasion many serious accidents, but still the 'amor pecuniae' overcomes all apprehensions and they are ready to face death itself for the acquisition of a few shillings more than usual wages of a labouring man.

August 29th

After breakfast this morning I crossed the water to South Shields and walked from thence to Sunderland seven miles distant. The principal object of my excursion was to examine the bridge of cast iron thrown across the river Wear, and indeed, I had every reason to be satisfied with the sight of this stupendous monument of human ingenuity and power, though the road was very uninteresting and disagreeable conducting me to it. It is only about four years ago since this great work was completed under the patronage of Mr. Burden, Member for the County. The arch of the bridge, for it consists of only one arch, ascends by easy ascent from one bank of the river Wear to the other, runs in span 236 feet. This is formed of bars of iron strongly fastened together and resting at each end on a stone pier. The height from the middle of the arch to the water is 100 feet; thus the largest vessels employed in the coal trade can go up the river to load without lowering their top-gallant masts. Iron rails and lampposts are carried along the passage across the bridge; in the centre on each side is this inscription "NIL DESPERANDUM AUSPICE DEO". I must confess I was rather disposed to cavil at this and think one more appropriate might be chosen, for although all human enterprises are under the direction of the Almighty in a work of this kind which depends upon mechanical labour, the proprietors without doubt trusted more to their mathematical calculations than upon divine assistance for their success. Thus it seems rather out of the way to introduce a religious sentiment into this place, and the rule of Horace might be applied in the present instance with some reason "NEC DEUS INTERSIT NISI DIGNUS VINDICE NODUS INCIDERET" but we must not be critics where the intention was so praiseworthy and the execution of it so truly beneficial. The expense attending the erection of the bridge was £30,000 to defray which a toll is collected from the foot passengers as well as carriages. I understand the town is built on each side of the river in the manner of Shields and does not seem superior in one respect; like the latter place it depends upon the coal trade for its support, and the inhabitants cannot be expected to have much time or taste for improvements.

The coast is very thinly scattered with trees, but some good corn is grown close to the sea. About two miles from South Shields there is an extensive view of the Tyne as far as Newcastle.

I returned to dinner after a walk of fourteen miles. N.B. The stone arch at Pontypridd, Glamorgan, is 144 ft. in span.

August 30th . . . SHIELDS
Walked this morning to Newcastle, eight miles to the West of this place; the road to it by no means abounds in picturesque objects; coal works and rope houses bespeak the activities and commercial enterprises of the inhabitants, but there are a few gentlemen's seats to adorn the country. One indeed I observed to the right, about a mile from Newcastle, a good, substantial stone-built building belonging to Mr. Mathew White.

The town of Newcastle is much in the same style as Shields. The streets are narrow, and the houses generally speaking, old and well built. A bridge over the river connects the buildings on each side of the water. Very little remains of the Castle; what was probably part of the keep, a heavy square structure, is now so much surrounded by houses I could take no sketch of it which otherwise I should have done, and as there seemed nothing particularly to interest my attention, I quitted the place a little after one o'clock and returned to Shields.

August 31st . . . SHIELDS
Having learned that Warkworth hermitage about twenty miles to the northward was well worthy of notice, also Alnwick, the seat of the Duke of Northumberland, I determined to visit them before I traced the Roman Wall from Newcastle to Carlisle. I therefore left my portmanteau in charge of Mrs. Carr at the Inn, and putting some things in a knapsack quitted Shields at 12 o'clock and proceeded along the coast four miles to Hartley, a small place but of late years rendered more important by a harbour formed in solid rock at the expense of my Lord Delaval who has a very fine mansion and estate half a mile distant. From hence they ship coal immediately from the pit, as the vessels may lie close to the rock which forms an excellent quay. This, I imagine is a very important saving, and must be of material advantage to the Estate. Beyond this, as I walked along the shore I was tempted by the smoothness of the sand to bathe here, but had occasion to repent it afterward as I was very ill the whole evening, so that I was constrained to remain at Blyth and was apprehensive of being detained on my route. However, finding myself better in the morning I proceeded after breakfast towards Warkworth.

September 1st . . . BLYTH
Not being quite strong, I procured a boy to carry my knapsack from Blyth to Newbiggin, a very pleasant walk for four miles along the smooth sand; indeed this part of the coast almost the whole way from Tynemouth is the finest for bathing I ever saw. Newbiggin stands on a little bay, on the north-east extremity of which is built a church which apparently in former times was of much larger dimensions. The chancel being suffered to go to decay, duty is only performed here now once a month, but the inhabitants attend service at Woodhorn half a mile distant. It is supposed that many

buildings extended beyond the church, but suffered from the encroachments of the sea which is by no means improbable as the name of Newbiggin seems to imply, that it rises from the ruins of a more ancient place.

Beyond the church I followed the coast for nearly a mile over a solid bed of rock very much resembling the pavement I had occasion to mention when at St. Donat's Castle, Glamorganshire. The surface is not so smooth, but the strata of the rock lie in a similar parallel direction, and at various distances are intercepted by narrow cliffs or channels through which the sea rushes with great violence and noise.

Returning, I made a sketch of the church and spent a very pleasant evening at the Inn where there is a boarding table kept for the company who come here to bathe at a guinea a week lodging. Included in the village are other lodging-houses apparently very comfortably fitted up let at the rate of six shillings a room. For a retired watering-place I think one cannot see a more pleasant situation; the sand is the finest imaginable, the air healthy, and the living very reasonable. The greatest inconvenience is the distance from a post-town, Morpeth being nearly eight miles off. Three bathing machines are kept here, and I understand that sometimes there is a great deal of company from Newcastle and the neighbourhood.

I was not a little pleased to get to a comfortable bed at eleven o'clock as I had not slept a wink the preceding night at Blyth, indeed it was with difficulty I got any shelter for the night as they refused to accommodate me at any of the Public Houses seeing I was ill.

September 2nd . . . NEWBIGGIN

Before breakfast this morning I walked to Woodhorn and sketched the church. The village is small and has nothing particularly worthy of notice, however I found myself much refreshed by my excursion and at 10 o'clock having taken leave of the party at the Inn from whom I had experienced much civility, I proceeded rather in a retrograde direction along the banks of the river Wansbeck in order to visit the remains of Bothel Castle which I understand are usually shewn to strangers. The walk to it ran through an interesting little valley of about five miles the scenery being diversified by wood and water presents many attractions for the pencil, but I was obliged to content myself with a sketch of the church and castle. I must confess my expectations had been too

much raised by a description I had heard of this antiquity, for very little remains of the ancient structure founded by the Bertram family. The gateway is evidently as late as the time of Elizabeth or perhaps even after, for the square casement windows were not in use (I believe) prior to her reign. A gardener who inhabits the gateway showed me two silver coins one of Henry VI the other of Elizabeth, at least I imagine them to be so but the inscriptions are much defaced. These were found a little time since as he was digging amongst the ruins which now enclose a good garden formed by the industry of this person who holds it of the Duke of Portland.

Quitting the castle, I walked a few steps to the clerk's house and got admittance to the church. This structure is entirely in the Welsh style without any tower or belfry, but probably there was something of the kind at its first erection. On entering the porch, I observed an ancient monument to the right lying even with the pavement. This was removed some years since from another part of the church. A cross sculptured in the Saxon manner and a sword represented near it, lead one to suppose it covered the grave of a Khan warrior, but the inscription, if there ever was any, has long since been defaced. There is a much more perfect monument but of a later date, on the right-hand side before you enter the chancel. This is formed of alabaster and represents a warrior and his lady in a recumbent posture. Under his feet is an animal something like an otter which my conductor informed me occasioned his death. A small animal resembling a rat is placed near the lady's foot on the folds of her drapery; the design of these inventions I cannot pretend to decipher. Under the head of the warrior is represented a bull's head most probably his crest; the lady reposes on a cushion supported by two little figures. Many other figures about six inches high representing nuns and monks are placed in niches round the side of the monument. Alas, the coat of arms, as I am no herald, I could not determine to whom it may belong. The castle was in the possession of the family of the Ogles for many generations which I learned from an inscription on the wall of the chancel, and it was probably a monument belonging to them. The sculpture is very superior to what one generally meets with, and it is rather to be lamented that a great part is hidden by the wainscotting of a pew adjoining.

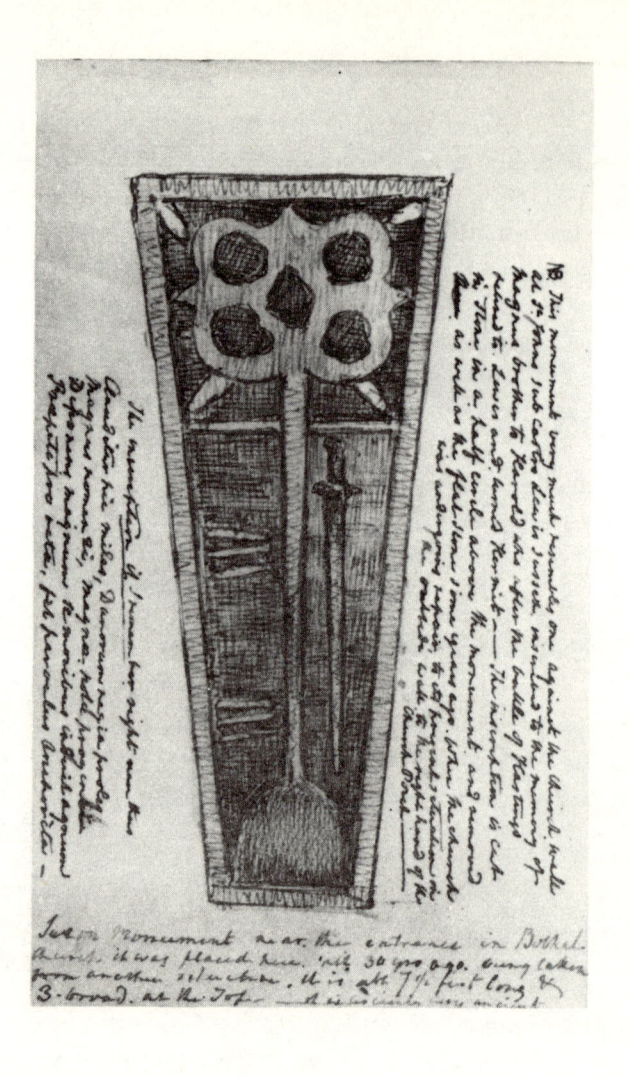

Leaving Bothel, I proceeded northwards to Warkworth. In my way I passed Widdrington where stood a castle in ancient times belonging to a family of that name; one of these is rendered immortal in the song of Chevy Chase. The old ruin was about twenty years ago entirely demolished and a modern mansion in castellated form erected on the spot. From thence to Warkworth I experienced a very dreary and uncomfortable walk, as the rain which had fallen very heavy earlier in the day, occasioned the road to become very dirty and slippery. However I was fortunate enough to get my knapsack carried by a man on horseback for the last five miles which was a great relief and saved my linen from a complete wetting which it was not in my power to avoid, for when I arrived at the place of my destination, there was not a dry thread on my back and I was obliged immediately to go to bed. This day's stage was about twenty miles.

September 3rd . . . WARKWORTH

Not being quite well this morning, I continued within doors till dinner-time employing my time in sketching with a pen, what I had pencilled yesterday. After dinner I walked to the Castle which is close to the Inn. This indeed is a noble monument of antiquity, and in respect to the size and situation, inferior to very few in the kingdom. The building is erected on very high ground, the west facing the river Coquet which winds in a serpentine direction through a picturesque valley. The east commands an extensive view of the ocean nearly a mile distant into which the same river empties itself. The small island of Coquet with an ancient chapel on the southern extremity, is seen just off the mouth of the river; this, and the white foam of the

Warkworth Castle from the River

breakers dashing against the shore attract the eye for a time before it ranges on the boundless space beyond. The walls of the castle are of hewn stone dug immediately on the spot; they extend in an irregular square along the high ground, the gateway towards the south defended by a trench. This was the only entrance, and seems to have been well fortified by two portcullis and a strong passage with openings for the discharge of missive weapons. In the area to the left are the remains of a large building having over the gateway in a square frame of stone, a mutilated lion and other armorial bearings of the Percies. At the northend is a very handsome regular structure, a wall 50 or 60 ft. high and a square tower of observation rising still higher. This in all probability contained the principal rooms of the Lords and their attendants; the other apartments in the Towers and over the Gateway were for the garrison and servants. It is very extraordinary that so little is known respecting this building on the spot however, I have not been fortunate enough to meet with any satisfactory account of its foundation and different proprietors. The Lords of Northumberland have held it for many ages, but whether it was originally built by them or not I am not informed. A servant is here maintained by the present Duke, and inhabits apartments near the Gateway. Before having made a circuit of the Castle he attended me along the banks of the river to a boat of which he had charge for the convenience of the company visiting the Hermitage a hundred yards up the water. Had the weather favoured me I should have delighted in this excursion, for the scenery possesses innumerable beauties; the Castle with its lofty

East view of Warkworth Castle

walls receding as you advance, giving place to sloping hills covered with verdure; the clear stream beset with various coloured foliage of the trees adorning the banks, and here and there a jutting rock presents a fine relief to the darker shades that surround it.

The Hermitage is cut in the cliff of freestone rising a few yards above the water, and from the boat, rising by an easy ascent to the ruins of a small building said to have been the residence of the Hermit. Above this a door opens into an apartment called the Chapel, about 18 ft. long, 7 ft. broad and the same in height, built in solid stone, pillars with arches crossing at the roof give relief and ornament to the interior. Two small Gothic apertures afford a melancholy view well adapted to contemplation. At the further end, part of the stone is left square with a small cornice to it about 3 ft. high which was the altar. Above this is a little Gothic niche probably contained a crucifix, but what most excites the curiosity is a kind of monument to the right of the altar on which is represented a female figure lying in a recumbent posture with an ancient person at her feet. Tradition and the ballad pretend that this was sculptured by direction of the Hermit in remembrance of the lady of his affections whom he destroyed through mistaken jealousy, and was the occasion of his renouncing the world. To make this more intelligible I will, at my leisure transcribe the legend as given by Dr. Percy. Beyond the chapel are two smaller apartments communicating with it by a Gothic door lighted by a window, if it can be called a light, which the poet described as only rendering darkness more visible. Over the door on an escutcheon are carved emblems of the Crucifixion: this is much defaced, and the inscription which is round it is entirely so. In one of the further apartments a square is left resembling the altar in the chapel, but for what it was designed I cannot pretend to determine. So much was I struck with this spot that I shall endeavour to be better acquainted with it, and shall accordingly prolong my stay here in order to occupy a few hours this evening. I will begin to transcribe the poem* relating to this Hermitage, and on my second visit I hope to enter more fully into the minutiae of this singular little antique.

September 4th

It rained the whole of this morning which gave me an opportunity of finishing this long poem; the story certainly might be better told. Such as it is, I am indebted to it for some hours employment which otherwise might have hung heavy on my hands. I should have preferred meeting with more authentic record of the Hermitage, but I know not where it is to be found and therefore must be satisfied with the labour of today and trust to the invention of others rather than my own. Sir Bertram was one of the Lords of Bothel Castle which I visited the day before yesterday, and it is thought that some of the family endowed Brinkburn Priory and built Brinkshaugh Chapel both in the same valley higher up the river. The name of Sir Bertram (or Bertrand) is rendered famous for that beautiful fragment of Mrs. Aikens' more calculated to inspire sentiment of superstitious awe than all the threadbare descriptions of Mrs. Radcliffe or the absurd nonsense of Mr. Lewis.

September 5th

This morning proving very fine, I soon began my excursion and was very occupied till dinner-time in taking sketches of the castle, and in again visiting the Hermitage; indeed, the greater part of the time was spent at the latter place, for the keys and the boat were entrusted to me, and the gloomy solemnity of the place possessed me.

September 7th

My knapsack proving too heavy, I forwarded it by the Shields carrier and only took a change of linen with me. The weather was more favourable, and I left my Inn at Warkworth, and proceeding along the banks of the Coquet to the west, experienced a very interesting walk for eight miles to Felton, a small place standing on the Northern road. I had been informed of an ancient Abbey some miles up the river which occasioned my present deviation instead of returning direct to Shields. As it was too far to reach this evening I determined to take up my abode in my present quarters, and was more induced in this determination by the civility and attention of my host who had been a soldier in the American War where he had lost an arm and an eye. After dinner he accompanied me a little tour round the village and along the side of the river. Being a good trout fisher, every turning and shallow of the stream possessed some particular attraction to his mind, and I was much amused by his conversation and remarks on other subjects which were far above what I should have expected from one in his station, – what is more bespoke a good heart. In the evening on my return to the Inn I found a party assembled from the harvest field, and having procured a blind fiddler, were preparing for a dance. As my object is to observe everything, I went upstairs and saw a great many Scotch reels danced with great life and spirit however different they might have been in grace and elegance, but the dancers not breaking up till past one o'clock, from necessity I was obliged to sit up in the parlour, the scene of amusement being too close to the room allotted for my sleeping apartment.

* This has 806 lines and has been omitted. Ed.

I have met with a very sensible man who I at first took to be a clergyman but afterwards found he was steward to a Mr. Davidson a gentleman in the neighbourhood. On mentioning my intention of viewing the ruins of Brinkburn Abbey, he readily offered to accompany me the next morning; as he was well acquainted with the place, I accepted his proposal with pleasure. N.B. There is a very large society in this part of the country amongst gentlemen of extensive property.

September 8th
Walked to Brinkburn Abbey in company with Mr. Atkinson the person before mentioned, and was much gratified by his observations which disclosed much reading and reflection. In our walk we passed a Roman road crossing the higher ground above the Coquet, and running to the northward. This pavement in some places is quite perfect, composed of large square stones, the passages being 8 ft. in breadth. This is part of Watling Street. From this high ground covered with mounds and entrenchments, we suddenly looked down upon the Abbey built close to the foot of the hill having the river in front, and is so completely hidden in a narrow vale that it can be seen from no spot 200 yards distant from it. As this situation afforded a good bird's eye view of the tower and aisles, I first sketched the ground plan before I surveyed the exterior of the building. It is cruciform, very much resembling Tintern Abbey but of much smaller dimensions and of less elegant architecture. It seems to be in length about 200 ft. and a little more than half as much across aisles, but for some reason the four archways on which the tower formerly stood, are now filled up with strong built walls dividing the building into four parts. The partition walls are of great solidity and strength, and seem to have stood many years. The pillars are very heavy, for the most part resembling the ancient Saxon style though the windows are pointed. It is said this

was founded by one of the Bertram family about the time of Edward I, but I should imagine it was more ancient. In the Civil Wars it was converted into a hospital by the Parliamentary troops. In respect to situation, there cannot be one more calculated for monastic retirement; – a beautiful river washed its walls to the south, a verdant hill rising behind defended it from the north, to the east and west the river banks covered with wood, afforded good shelter as well as ornament. In a straight line it is not more than ten miles from the sea from whence the monks derived their foreign supplies.

Just above the Abbey on higher ground was one of the strongest posts in the country for a refuge in time of troubles. The mounds, trenches and earthworks (still to be traced in every direction) show that the natural advantages of the situation had been improved by art, but whether they were formed by the Romans who certainly had many stations in the neighbourhood, or whether they were afterward raised as defence against the Scots in their intrusions, by the inhabitants of this county, I cannot pretend to determine. The Roman road crossed the river near this place and extended as before mentioned along this high ground towards the north. This would lead us to suppose they had been well acquainted with the situation and very probably might have raised some works here. About five miles to the south-east is a large square entrenchment attributed to them, but the situation is by no means so advantageous for an encampment as the ground above the Abbey. Having taken two sketches, one of the northern the other of the southern front, I returned by the banks of the river to Felton after a walk of a good many miles, it being nearly six o'clock on my return to the Inn which I had quitted at nine.

September 9th

At 7'o'clock this morning I left Felton and proceeded along the turnpike road to Morpeth . . . 11 miles. This is an inconsiderable place in itself but is remarkable for being the greatest market for cattle in the kingdom next to Smithfield; dealers coming out of Scotland and York to attend it, and frequently many thousand head are sold in a day. Beyond the bridge which crosses the Wansbeck are some artificial mounds where formerly stood the Castle; having the river in front must have been a very strong position. Very little of the remains are now to be seen.

I did not stop at Morpeth, but taking the road to the left of the bridge endeavoured to make the shortest cut to Shields, but afterwards regretted I did not continue the turnpike to Newcastle, a few miles further but I am convinced less fatiguing than the mirey road I chose. After walking about seven miles I was obliged to rest at a small ale-house by the roadside for nearly an hour. I have heard more of the Northumbrian dialect than I had before met with; it appears to be Scotch. A little girl was rocking a child in a cradle in the house, and on my enquiring whether the host was at home and whose child it was, she told me "the bairn" belonged to her mistress; that "the guid man" was dead; that the mistress was "ganged down the burn and would not be hame yet"; that "the laddie and lassie before the door" were her mistress's and many other expressions perfectly Scottish.

I arrived at Shields a little after six in the evening and took up my quarters at the Inn I had before put up at; indeed I was not a little glad to get to bed after a walk of above 28 miles. I forgot to mention a singular quarrel I was witness to between two butchers returning from Morpeth market; the expressions they made use of, and the manner in which they conducted their abuse reminded me of Horace's voyage and will not bear repetition, but poor human nature did not appear to advantage I must confess. I left when he drew his picture of the Yahoo, [and he] would not have been sorry to have borrowed some materials from such a source.

September 10th
I was under the necessity of spending this day at Shields as my things were not arrived from Warkworth. In the morning I was shown the Lifeboat purposely built for saving sailors in distress. I little thought it might be called for so shortly after. In the evening about six o'clock, a boat with seven persons was overset endeavouring to cross the bar and all were drowned excepting a boy, for no assistance could be procured in time. Not half-an-hour before I had been myself in a small wherry close to the bar and found very little swell, but it afterwards increased so much as to fill the boat which sank immediately. [*Ed:* There follow extracts from Camden respecting the Roman work.]

September 11th . . . Excursion along the Roman Wall
At a little after nine this morning I left Shields in order to begin my observations on the remains of the Roman Wall. After walking four miles on the Newcastle turnpike, I turned down to the left to a small place consisting of a few houses inhabited by colliers called Wallsend. A gentleman from Newcastle, a Mr. Armstrong whom I had met at Shields accompanied me to the house of a Mr. Buddle, who he informed me was better acquainted with the antiquities on the spot than any other person, and indeed I was much indebted to him for his remarks and attention. Near his house are the visible traces of a regular square enclosure 130 yds. each way, this was covered with buildings. As it is scarcely possible to dig anywhere in this area without coming to the

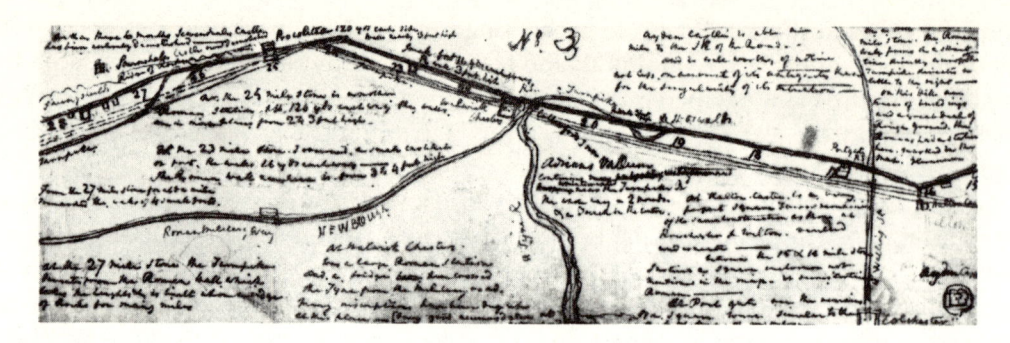

foundations, not a long time since whilst making addition to Mr. Buddle's dwelling house, they discovered a circular hole sunk in the ground, neatly paved at the sides and at the bottom. It was 9 ft. in diameter, above the same in depth, but only 2½ ft. wide at the bottom. This was nearly filled with burnt earth or ashes and the bones of animals. They have preserved the antlers of a very large stag, being above 2 ft. long, also the skull of a goat and a small cow or ox with other parts of animals' skeletons used in sacrifice.

Mr. Buddle also showed me many pieces of Roman pottery dug up at different times, two or three of these fragments I endeavoured to sketch as they appeared to be more highly finished than the rest. The largest piece has a figure on it representing, I imagine, a slave carrying a burthen on his head, and a female figure with a cornucopia is not so distinct. The border round the upper part is very elegant. This square was no doubt a fortress or station at the extremity of the Wall continually garrisoned by soldiers. A wall or pier running from the south-east side of the square was quite visible a year ago, and very large stones belonging to its foundations were taken out of the river on account of their being obstructive to the vessels coming to the colliery. This cross wall was possibly designed to prevent the enemy passing the fortress at low water which they otherwise might have done.

Leaving Mr. Buddle's house I followed the course of the Wall running west to Newcastle. Very little of it is to be seen excepting a gentle rise about a foot and a half high through the two first fields I passed. Ascending the rising ground towards a windmill, the trench is more visible. Just about where the footpath leads into the turnpike at Byker Hill, they are now employed in digging up the foundations of the Wall to clear the ground of the stones. This gave me an opportunity of seeing it more plainly, for hitherto I had only observed a kind of earth-mound here, and I could trace the position of the stones at the bottom. Some of them were very large, but as there are quarries on the spot they had not far to carry them. From Byker Hill to the entrance of Newcastle the ground has been so much built over I could see nothing of the course of the Wall, nor indeed is it with certainty known what direction it took to Westgate.

I dined at Newcastle with Mr. Armstrong, and though much gratified by his politeness it occasioned a very material delay and I was not on my way again until nearly five o'clock. This gentleman accompanied me to Westgate but through mistake I took the road to Benwell to the left, instead of following the direct Carlisle road which runs on the very foundation of the Wall. However it gave me the opportunity of seeing a very pretty village and a large mansion belonging to Mr. Bowes which unfortunately is going to ruin. I gained the turnpike again about two miles from Newcastle and walked forward to Denton Burn, a few houses standing on each side of the road. A mile beyond here it was, I first saw the wall above ground if I may so express it. A small part stands in a field a few yards to the left of the turnpike having an apple-tree growing on the western extremity. It may be about 30 ft. long, 8 or 9 ft. wide, and 3 ft. high and has this appearance [drawing].* It is nowhere visible from Newcastle until you come to this place. On the hill beyond Denton Burn the mound and trench are higher and deeper than I have before observed; the road runs close to them, but after a few hundred yards they are no longer visible. The farmers are at work upon this mound also, the same as at Byker Hill and have grubbed up some very large stones. Soon every trace will be lost from Newcastle as far as I have yet proceeded. The Antiquary may regret it, but still in the course of things it must be so, and the whole globe itself must dissolve and like the baseless fabric of a vision leave not a trace behind. The evening began to close in soon after I passed Denton and I had eight miles further to walk to Harley-on-the-Hill before I stood a chance of procuring a bed. However, there was no alternative, and I marched forward with as much expedition as possible.

At Haddon-on-the-Wall where I stopped to inquire the distance, I was insulted by a drunken fellow who declared I was a spy; of course I took no notice of him and left him drinking in the ale-house. However, half an hour after he overtook me on the road and behaved in such a manner I really thought I would have come to close quarters, but at length he passed on full gallop. Whether this man had prejudiced the people against me, or whether they might not of themselves give into this man's ideas I am yet to learn, but on my arrival at the Inn at Harley at 10 o'clock, they received me in such a curious manner that my feelings overcame my interest and I left the house. Fortunately for me there was another public house in the village, and more fortunately they did not conceive such uncharitable ideas respecting a benighted traveller; I have found civil treatment and a comfortable bed, which after fatigues of the day having walked about 20 miles, was not undeserved.

September 12th . . . HARLEY HILL

Having passed over the great part of the road in the dark last night, I determined to take up my quarters here for a day (that is, my sleeping quarters), and return to beyond Haddon-on-the-Wall in order to explore what I had been obliged to neglect. At Haddon I procured a person to attend me, and through his assistance was enabled to form the communication from where I left off in the evening.

From near Denton Burn as I have before observed, little of the Wall can be seen excepting here and there where the turnpike is worn, but at Walbottle a short distance from the road there are appearances of ancient buildings. The vallum of Adrian is here seen running in a parallel direction: a hundred yards distant from the Roman Wall, about a quarter of a mile before you come to Haddon-on-the-Wall close to the turnpike on the left hand, on a bank bounding the road, a piece of the Wall is very visible. It may be about 4 ft. high from the bank top. Though some of the stones have been removed, it still is of great thickness and the cement remarkably hard. I have remarked that the

---
* Drawing not reproduced—Ed.

foundation stones alone were wrought, those on the superstructure were all shapes and sizes apparently thrown into quicklime, as the cement seems to adhere very closely to every part, and the outside stones removed from the spot probably were squared as at Denton Burn. The road deviates a little from the wall at Haddon, and some of the houses on the rising ground to the left are built on its foundation. In a farmer's rickyard on this bank I perfectly traced the groundwork of the Wall composed of square stones just 8 ft. wide; from what I had hitherto observed it seems that when the turnpike was made (which was just after the Rebellion in '45), they followed the Wall as closely as possible where they could do it with advantage, and only deviated from it on the rising ground where the ascent was too steep. Thus it happened that more is to be seen on hills and eminences than on the level country. To the south of the road a little distance from Haddon Church a short time since, a man found a large iron wedge and two silver coins while forming the new turnpike to Hexham. I had sufficient curiosity to visit the spot, and the exact place was shewn to me by a person who was present. It is on the side of a steep bank, and might have been the site of one of the original Forts erected by Agricola. On enquiring for the coins of the man who discovered them I found one had been given to Mr. Ellison, vicar of the place, the other, which he had broken in two in digging, was lost. Mr. Ellison being unfortunately from home I could not procure sight of this. I was equally unsuccessful in not seeing a large silver coin in possession of an old woman who found it in a field near Rowchester. The inscription on this, my conductor informed me, was very perfect.

At Turpin's Hill about a mile to the north of the road some years ago, a poor man discovered a large earthen jar full of gold coins at least it is supposed so. Two or three he gave to his landlord, the rest it is imagined, he sold at Newcastle to a goldsmith as he was well supplied with money for sometime after. A poor woman still living at Haddon sold to a goldsmith some gold and silver coins for which she received £5, in all probability a third of their real value considered as bullion, but perhaps inestimable to the antiquarian; these without doubt were melted.

Tracing the Wall in part along the turnpike from Haddon where the foundation stones are seen sometimes 20 ft. in length, I came to Rowchester now a farm house near the road, where my guide assured me I should get a sight of some of the coins as a vast number had been found by the farmer a Mr. Bargus. The farmer was at home and very civil, but the coins he had disposed of to his landlord, by the account he gave, many were of Vespasian. Although disappointed in respect to one kind of antique, I had much scope for observation in walking in the fields round his house. Here evidently was a very large Roman station as the name Chester implies. An equilateral square containing four acres surrounded by a trench is easily traced, strong walls defend it on all sides. About sixty yards of the square projected beyond the direction of the Roman Wall to the north, and a much greater extent was contained within it. Almost the whole of this area the farmer assured me, on his coming to live there, was covered with stones, the foundations of houses many of great magnitude. Although he had endeavoured to clear them during that time, to mend the roads and repair walls, still, thousands of cartloads may still be procured from thence. To the west of the square not long ago, in clearing away the rubbish, they came to a stone trough cut in the solid rock. This they emptied of the earth and dirt it contained and found an iron candlestick standing on three legs, and a small bone he called a toothpick. I measured the dimensions of the trough which is now perfectly cleaned to the bottom, and found it 11 ft. long, 4 ft. wide and 2½ ft. deep. At one corner was an aperture for carrying off the water. This might have been a reservoir for water, as I scarcely think it was deep enough for a bath and there is no appearance of its having ever been higher at the sides.

The south end of the farmer's dwelling house is formed of a square tower formerly standing by itself. The stones of the walls are of a great size some being nearly a yard long, 2 ft. over, the walls themselves above 4 ft. thick. Two or three flat Roman tiles such as I observed at the small tower of Dover Castle are let in between the stones; without doubt this was a part of the original fortress, but it must have undergone some alterations as a kind of Gothic window now stopped up, is in the western wall. The doorway to the north may also be traced, the arch formed by two solid stones; this is now filled up. The farmer informed me within his remembrance there was a Roman Catholic chapel near the farm, and it is more than probable that this place contained many inhabitants even in later times. That part of it originally suffered by fire is evident from the burnt wood and black earth they dug up in many places, also masses of lead ran in and became encrusted with the earth.

Could we recall past scenes this identical spot might appear conspicuous amongst the devoted habitations of the Britons when their protectors left them to the ravages of the barbarians. Those buildings now in ruins perhaps once echoed with the groans of the suffering victims who neither found safety in flight, in arms, or in submission. Far better is it that the pacific ploughshare should pass over these walls than they should ever again become witness to the horrors of war, but in the rotation of human concerns, what changes may not happen; what have not happened to our knowledge? Who would have imagined that the British thunder should ever be heard on the banks of the Nile; that the Egyptians, once the conquerors and the instructors of the world, should disintegrate into a herd of slaves? What has become of the Romans? With what contempt do we regard these reputed barbarians who crouched to them for protection, now look upon the helpless Italians! In the course of a few centuries, what may not be the fate of this great and wealthy nation we inhabit? The fall of various kingdoms and empires teaches humility while it excites our admiration; indeed we can only wonder as we pass on, at the design of Providence beyond our comprehension, and it is folly to attempt the investigation further than is connected with our immediate improvements. I returned to dinner at 4 o'clock at Harley Hill and continued within doors writing until bedtime.

September 13th
Quitted Harlow Hill a little after nine, and passing along the turnpike road for about half a mile, turned off a little to the left in order to explore Welton (a few houses standing on the rising ground about a quarter of a mile from the road). The name Welton, which is evidently a corruption of Walltown, made me imagine I might trace some remains of an ancient station, but nothing now is to be seen but a square tower converted into a dwelling house. The walls are above a yard in thickness, and a winding flight of steps ascends to the top; in a loft above there is a communication door formed the same as the one I noticed at Rowchester, two solid stones making the

arch, and under the tower there is an arched cellar. Near the farm, on top of the steps made for mounting a horse, there is a stone 2½ ft. long, 2 ft. wide and 6 inches thick. On the west end is this inscription . . . LEG: 11 . . . AUG F, this was taken by the farmer a little time since, from the foundation of a square fort to the south of the Wall. The inscription I think, commemorates that the 2nd Legion founded the fort. The stone was certainly larger, but was broken in conveying it to the present situation.

A little beyond the turning off to Welton, Adrian's trench seems much wider and inclined nearer to the road. From Wallhouses, a few scattered buildings on the side of the road to the turnpike gate – nearly a mile, Severus' trench is quite perfect, about 40 or 50 ft. wide and shelving on each side until it meets at the bottom 8 ft. deep. This part, having formerly been covered with wood has suffered less than where cultivation has been more prevalent. Hadrian's vallum about 50 yards to the left of the turnpike house is also more visible than I have yet observed it. There is evidently here a double mound and the trench in the middle. This appearance continues for many miles and in a much more perfect state than towards Newcastle. A little beyond Halton Shields (a few scattered houses by the roadside) on ascending the rising ground, the foundation of the Roman Road is visible for some way where the turnpike is worn. Near the 15 milestone the turnpike deviates a little to the right from the straight course of the Roman Wall, passes direct over the hill for about 200 yards before it again meets the road.

The Romans in their work seem to have been too proud to have suffered even natural impediments to divert them from their purpose, and though they might have turned the Wall at the foot of the hill, they preferred going straight over it. On the top and sides of the hill to the south, are traces of buildings as this was too important a spot to pass unnoticed, and in all probability there was a station of some importance. The whole of the hill, about a quarter of a mile in circumference, consists of broken ground some part standing like detached hillocks or barrows. One to the south end, which they are now digging to procure stones for the road, presents a very singular appearance. It may be about 30 ft. in diameter and 15 ft. in depth, the labourers having conveyed away nearly half of it. A section is formed for observation, for about 2 ft. from the surface there is a thick stratum of small limestones cemented together just in the same manner as the interior of the Roman Wall. Below this are larger stones thrown in various directions, some edgeways, some flat, some quite square as if wrought for the facing of a building. Beneath this are very large stones forming the foundations having visibly the same kind of cement between them. At first I naturally imagined that this hillock was occasioned by very large ruins of buildings fallen together, but on walking further from the spot I everywhere remarked the same appearances quite to the summit of the hill, the small stones being invariably at the surface. A little reflection convinced me that had it been the base of walls and buildings the surface would not have exhibited the same kind of incrustations, but that larger kinds of stones would also be mixed with the smaller.

Mr. Bates, who afterwards accompanied me to this spot endeavoured to account for this phenomenon by suggesting the whole hill is composed of limestone and might sometime or other have experienced a volcanic heat that ran some of the stones into this kind of cement; I must confess I did not think the solution satisfactory and must leave the hill as I found it for the investigations of those who are better skilled than myself. Whatever this may have been, there are vestiges in different places of walls and buildings especially to the south, and indeed Hadrian's vallum forms a double trench of some depth at the foot of the hill, and running to the west, loses itself for some distance in the meadow ground beneath. To the south east side of the hill I traced a square embankment about two feet above the ground in which I conjecture there was formerly a wall, and the enclosure used for securing cattle in case of alarm when the enemy appeared upon the lines.

I walked across the fields from this hill to an old farmhouse bearing the name of Halton Castle, for I heard at Harlow one of the most perfect square towers in the neighbourhood was to be seen here, and indeed I was not disappointed. On requesting permission to view it, Mr. Bates the tenant very hospitably received me and conducted

me over the tower which now is converted into part of the dwelling house. We first visited a vault beneath the building. This is arched over in the same manner as the one I saw at Welton; above this is a square room used as a storeroom; the window to it gave me an opportunity of seeing the thickness of the walls these being considerably above 4 ft. A modern bedroom is lately made over this apartment, but very properly in papering it they had not covered two niches in the wall used two or three centuries ago for Holy water, the Roman Catholic family who then inhabited the place having converted it into a chapel. Ascending some stone steps I was conducted through a pigeon house to the roof of the tower. Indeed, independently of antiquaries' investigations I had reason to be pleased with the trouble I had taken on account of the fine prospect viewed from this eminence. Mr. Bates had pointed out to me the spot where formerly stood the house of the unfortunate Lord Derwentwater who suffered in the Rebellion of '15. This is about 5 miles distant on the further bank of the Tyne. His estates producing £20,000 per annum were forfeited to the Crown and afterwards bestowed on Greenwich Hospital.

The town of Hexham and the village of Corbridge are about the same distance on the borders of the Tyne which flows through a most highly cultivated country in a beautiful and enchanting direction. Beyond this, the view is shut in by very high ground where there are lead mines producing very considerably and employing some hundreds of people. My conductor also pointed out the situation of Prudhoe Castle, now in ruins, Corchester a large Roman station through which passed Watling Street, the road to the north, and Aydon Castle not above a mile distant, supposed to be a Roman fortress.

Having admired the distant view I turned my observation to objects nearer home. At each corner of the tower is a little circular turret or rather projection, as they do not rise above the battlements; these are formed with very neat masonry but I was astonished to see such large stones employed at the top of the building which could not have been done had the wall been of less solid materials. Here and there between the joining of the squares I removed pieces of Roman tiles. Descending the tower my host insisted upon my dining with him and promised afterwards to accompany me to Aydon Castle the habitation of his father who rents nearly a thousand acres under Mr. E. Blackett.

Aydon Castle is certainly most deserving the attention of the antiquary, and it is not less remarkable on account of age than it is for the strength and singularity of its position. The outward walls enclosing nearly two acres are built on the brink of a steep rock or peninsula above 150 ft.; perpendicular above a brook which nearly encircles it at the bottom. Very steep banks covered with woods rise at an equal height with the castle rock about 200 ft. beyond forming a deep breach or chasm of that width and about 150 ft. in depth. For two thirds of the circumference of the castle there was no possible approach but by the neck of this peninsula where is the entrance, and this was through a narrow gateway under a plain wall of great strength and thickness facing the west circular tower. To the north west angle is a semi-circular tower formed of prodigious stones, so indeed is the whole of the outward wall beneath which is a dungeon as I have endeavoured to describe in my sketch. The walls of this part are immensely thick and the tower was apparently once very high. The dwelling to the south east angle is, I think more modern than the outward walls, and is formed of a harder kind of stone very neatly squared. Some of the windows are pointed in this part of the edifice but the openings in walls are shaped in the manner I have described. On the opposite side, the stables are I believe, unique of their kind being arched over like the vault of a cellar and having the mangers of wrought stone. There was a chapel added to the dwelling-house to the south but is now broken away, – I wish very much to see some account of this building for it appears to me originally a work of the Romans who well knew the importance of such a situation so near the line of their station.

After having conducted me to every part of this ancient structure which nevertheless is a good dwelling-house, Mr. Bates wished to occupy my attention by objects of another kind, and taking me across the fields, showed me in a very rich pasture some of the largest Leicestershire sheep I ever beheld. These begin to be universally sought in this part of the country, for it is discovered that one of this kind will thrive as much in a year on the same feed as another would do in three; of course the profit must be very great to the feeder. He also breeds a great many cattle from the northern breeds crossed with the Lincolnshire. The young man who occupies as much land as his father, namely one thousand acres, assured me he valued the stock on his farm at 7,000 guineas. This gave one a little idea of the extensive scale on which agriculture is here conducted. He is now erecting a threshing mill to work by water not far from his house, which when complete will cost above £600.

When talking of cattle, Mr. Bates gave me a curious account of the original breed of the north which is now only preserved at Lord Tankerville's. The cows and bulls are white excepting the tips of their ears and tails, and a good deal smaller than what we generally see in the south. They herd together, and are exceedingly fierce. If a stranger approaches they come up to him in a body, wheel round, stamp with their feet and menace with their horns. In a short space they set off from him full gallop, make another circle and approach much nearer. They repeat the same procedure perhaps a third time, and if the intruder does not make his retreat in good earnest, he stands a chance of being very roughly used. The cow hides her calf as soon as it is dropped and no-one dares come near it. If one of the herd is sick or wounded, the rest goad him by trampling him to death. (I could make a simile but will forbear!)

My hospitable conductor insisted on my spending the evening with him, and before I left I met his brother who had just returned from the Highlands. He shewed me a grammar of the Erse language which he had brought home with him, also a Testament and book of poems, – the poems of Ossian he says, and so far from being neglected or forgotten, there are many people who can repeat the greatest part of the original at the present day, and it constitutes one of their favourite amusements so to do. I have never met with the controversy on the subject but it appears very extraordinary that it should have been extended so far, seeing how soon it might be decided. After a day fully and pleasantly occupied, I got to bed about 12 o'clock.

September 14th

On rising this morning, I took a drawing of the house and square tower. After breakfast Mr. Bates showed me three Roman coins dug up on the spot, one a silver coin of Hadrian, the two others of Magentius and Constantius. If I remember right after the death of Constantine the Great these two were contending rivals in power until finally the whole empire vested in Constantius. It is singular their effigies should be found so near each other, apt emblems of Death which permits no distinction in the grave, where friends and foes, mighty and weak, wise and foolish, mingle in one common dust. Mr. Bates had also a brass coin representing the figure of an angel killing a dragon (meant for the devil I suppose). Round the rim were many Saxon letters or so they appeared but I could not attempt to guess the inscription especially the Ā and Θ. My sketches being finished, Mr. Bates accompanied me to a Roman square enclosure near the road that appears to have been about 100 yards in breadth, 150 yards in length having four entrances. Stones have been dug from hence with inscriptions but are now destroyed. From hence we walked about 1½ miles along the turnpike to the 17 milestone where we turned off to Portgate, another station not so large nor so visible as the former. Here has been a square tower like that of Halton, Welton and Rowchester but it now forms the centre of an outhouse to the farm. The door is exactly the same on the outside as those before noted. One on the inside is square like those at Aydon Castle. Beyond this farm on the rising ground is held annually the largest fair for cattle in the kingdom.

Returning to the turnpike, I took leave of my obliging conductor and proceeded forward to Collerford Inn 5 miles distant, the place of my destination for the night, as I had much to insert in my diary. After walking about a mile and a half ascending a gentle hill over which the road passes, I clearly traced for many yards together the foundations of the Wall, where the turnpike was worn. The land on each side here begins to assume a less cultivated appearance, consequently the trenches are more distinct and Adrian's is not above 25 yards from the Wall. Before I came to the 18 milestone at Castle Studs, I endeavoured to trace the entrenchment but without success. Just beyond at the top of Cockley Hill some houses are built on the very foundations of the wall, the road here diverges some yards to the left and both Hadrian's and Severus's walls intersect a cornfield between St. Oswald's Chapel and the road. Descending the hill near where the turnpike again crosses the Wall, I was much gratified by seeing the original structure about 100 ft. in length above the ground in a grass field to the left. This is nearly 4 ft. high and the same breadth as before noted, 8 ft. The facing stones are wrought, and in some places the cement is quite solid on the outside. This part is, I understand to remain, but Mr. Clayton the proprietor has been sometime employed and is still employed in taking up the foundations on each side of it.

Collerford lies at the bottom of the hill on the other side of the bridge, and the Inn is a very comfortable house. After dinner I walked to Mr. Clayton's (a gentleman of Newcastle who has bought the estate in the neighbourhood of the Chesters). He was from home, but I was shewn some large stones with inscriptions lately taken from this station which probably was one of great importance in the line. By what I can observe, it extended above 200 yards each way, rising in a gentle ascent on the west side above the river having a bridge near where the Wall passed in a direct line down to it. Large masses of ruins rising in heaps over a spacious field speak of former greatness. Mr. Clayton has the column of a pillar well finished probably belonging to some public edifice, but in clearing the field, as they never go above two or three feet below the present surface, it is not to be expected that anything of importance will be discovered.

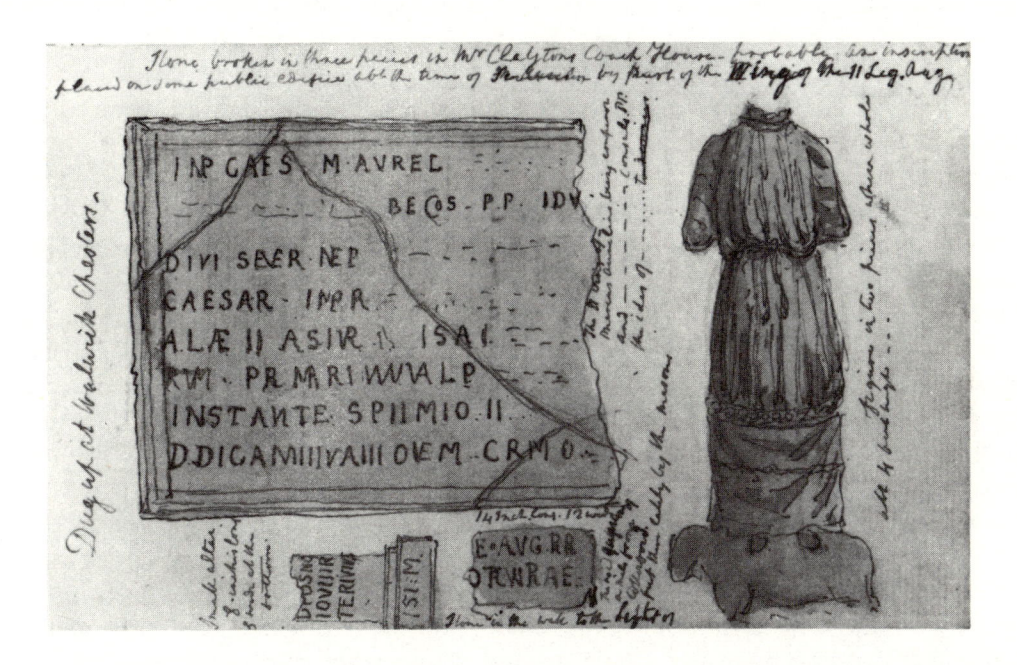

The mutilated figure of a woman standing on the back of some animal has lately been dug up and is at present put in a wall enclosing a plantation; I should think it deserved a better situation. Indeed, too little attention is paid to things of this sort in general, but here they seem particularly negligent, as some masons who were making a new wall near the turnpike confessed to me that they had broken up many large stones covered with inscriptions. One I saw casually placed in the wall. An antiquarian might really have a fine field for his researches if he were possessed of time and money to pursue them on this spot, I can only just skim the surface; occupation is my object but more knowledge is requisite in order to be at home in this kind of investigation. Indeed, those who are best skilled in Roman antiquities are often at a loss to hazard a conjecture on the mutilated remains of so many ages, and it would be presumption in me to attempt it where anything is left to conjecture.

September 15th
It was 11 o'clock before I left the Inn at Collerford, so much of my time being necessarily employed in arranging the occupation of the preceding day. The bridge of Collerford is a modern structure and passes over the north branch of the Tyne. The Inn stands close to it, and I have experienced better accommodation than I have yet met with, but a foot traveller ought never to complain. From a large map of North-umberland hanging in the dining-room I traced the Wall, which is of great service to

me. To the left way on the side of the road about ¼ mile from the Inn I copied the inscription of a stone placed lately in a new built wall by the masons; many others they informed me had been employed in this same way but without even the common attention of leaving the inscriptions on the outside. About ½ mile beyond this on the top of a hill above Walwick Chesters on passing a gentleman's seat, the Roman Wall appears running parallel to the turnpike 25 yards distant to the right. It is here in some places from 2–3 ft. above ground but mostly covered with earth and the facing stones gone.

Adrian's Vallum is close to the the road on the left, – just before I came to the 23 milestone I observed the traces of a small square adjoining the Roman Wall on the south side; the walls would seem to have been sixteen yards each way. This is the first of the small forts or castellets mentioned by Camden that I have seen.

Beyond this, the Wall is more perfect for nearly 200 yeards, about 3 ft. in height the breadth and facing entire. Mem: The Turnpike almost the whole of the way from Newcastle to the 23 milestone has hitherto been bounded by a stone wall on each side, here it is open. The country begins here to assume a more mountainous and barren appearance. About the 24 milestone the Turnpike which for 5 miles had deviated from the Wall, now again employs its foundations and continues on it for 3 miles. Adrian's Vallum runs quite close to the Roman Wall at the 24 stone and is cut very deep in the rock which is here close to the surface; for about 100 yards it seems to have been considered sufficiently strong in itself for Severus's trench is scarcely visible as though it had never been dug deep for that extent. Near the 25 milestone to the left of the road are the remains of one of the larger Roman Stations. It appears to have been 120 yards each way. The Wall to the south is formed of the same thickness as the Roman Wall and is still standing three feet above ground. This on the map is named Procolitia, – beyond this for nearly ¾ mile very little of either trench is visible, the ground being boggy.

At the 26th milestone the trenches are strongly marked on each side of the road. This country is here very barren in appearance, the hills covered with heath. At the 27 milestone the turnpike again deviates from the Wall which runs over a high ridge of rock for some miles from hence; following the Wall for about ¼ mile where it gradually ascends the heights I observed another of the small forts about 7 yards square on the south side of the Wall. About ½ mile beyond another the same size. Two hundred yards beyond this again, a larger, being ten yards square. Passing over a great deal of uneven ground I came to some houses where I enquired for Scavenshale Castle which formerly stood at the foot of this ridge of rocks, it is now entirely demolished but they pointed to the spot about a quarter of a mile distant.

As I continued following the course of the Wall which here runs upon an abrupt precipice 150 ft. high, I could not but remark the singular appearance of the rocks which rise up in square straight columns from the bottom fitted to each other so exactly that they appear rather the work of art than of nature. These are of the same kind as some stones I observed on the top of Cader Idris in Wales. One of these rocks had so singular an appearance that I stopped to sketch it, it rises nearly 40 ft. and on the top is the form of a rude armchair that seems a seat of pre-eminence few would contend for.

To the north of the ridge of rocks on a kind of boggy ground are four lakes, one of considerable extent nearly a mile in circumference, the other not so large; they informed me they abounded in pike and eels but I did not hear they contained trout. Between the houses I mentioned and the smaller lake called Craig, the most western of the four, I traced three other castellets two of 20 yards square, another of 5 yards, but at very irregular distances. I can by no means from what I have observed suppose there were stated, measured positions as mentioned in the account I have taken from Camden, but rather imagine the Romans built their forts according to the ground; had there been four smaller forts and one larger every mile surely it might have been known in these parts where the Wall still continues so perfect. In some places it is here 4 ft. high and 7 wide and continues in this state for many hundred feet together. But what most interested me of anything I have yet seen is a place called Housesteads or Borcovicus only one lone dwellinghouse is on the spot, and here I was sufficiently fortunate in procuring assistance in my researches from the inhabitants of the cottage and was shewn one of the most perfect inscriptions I have yet attempted to copy.

On this ground according to Camden stood a large Roman city. My expectations had been considerably excited and I thought if I could even walk over the ground selected by this powerful people for their principal station it would be a great satisfaction, and indeed in this respect I was fully gratified, for there are sufficient traces to shew the extent of the building and the prodigious thickness of the outer walls which enclose some acres on the side of the hills facing the south.

In the north it was defended by the Roman Wall running close to it. I fancied I could discover the four principal streets meeting in the centre. Be this as it may there are some remains that supposingly prove the magnificence of the buildings; many have been removed, but what treasures must be still buried beneath the ruins.

The first antique that occupied my attention was a large stone formerly an altar now employed to support the chimney at the cottage before-mentioned, unfortunately it has been so little regarded that other stones have been placed at the bottom so as to hide the inscription for the last two lines. The upper part is read thus, and clearly proves it a dedicatory altar to the titular Deities of the Augustan cohort by some of the stipendiaries quartered here commanded by Seoverius.

Surely there must be here as much scope for the observation of the antiquarian as any spot in the kingdom. How many hands might be employed during the winter when work is scarce, in digging the foundations!

The evening came in before I quitted the spot, and so much was I interested that even the calls of hunger were not attended to. It was about 8 when I arrived at the little Public House by the roadside and contrary to my expectations from the appearance of things, found a tolerable bed, but my hand pained me so much owing to a thorn broke in it some days ago that I could not sleep. The appellation of this place of entertainment is singular it being called 'Twice Brewed Ale'.

September 16th
It was above 12 o'clock before I had finished my writing and sketches. Then pursuing

my way across the turnpike I regained the higher ground over which the Roman Wall runs, nearly at the spot where I had before quitted it, that is, to the west of the small lake; from hence for nearly a mile little is to be seen of the original barrier, but a wall had been formed by the farmers on the foundation of the old one as a boundary. The original structure afterwards appears still higher than I have yet observed it, that is to say it measures nearly six feet on the south side, but on the other so many of the stones have rolled down the precipice that it is not above half its width and almost even with the rock. About three miles from the lake I traced another of the square forts 20 yards each way. This appears to have been divided towards the outer wall in this manner, the partitions seem to be too small for dwelling apartments, three of them being only 3 yards, the fourth 5 yards long. About a mile beyond this there is a steep descent from the ledge of rocks, and the Wall crosses a little brook that runs in the bottom and proceeding some way over the lower ground, – Adrian's trench which all along has kept the level ground about ¼ mile from Severus's (that is to say since the deviation of the turnpike at the 27 milestone) now approaches close to it.

A little way beyond on a gentle ascent is a square enclosure adjoining the Wall. This is called by the common people the Chesters; that is a strong fort or station as many so named are along the line. Here I must remark what no doubt has often been remarked before, that those places possessing the name of Chester or compounded with another name as Winchester, Colchester, Cirencester, Gloucester, and various others betoken some fort or station. The latin word *Castra* is perhaps the foundation of these derivations (and I must not get beyond my depth in matters of this kind).

The Chesters, according to the map, the station of Aesica, enclose about three acres of ground adjoining the Roman Wall to the north and was defended by a deep trench on the other sides. The walls are plainly traced the whole way and seem to have been the same thickness as the Roman Wall. There were three gateways, two facing each other on the East and West sides about fifteen feet from the Roman Wall, the other was to the southeast; foundations of buildings cover the whole of this area. Towards the centre is an underground archway about 5 ft. wide and 4 ft. high and as many in depth. When discovered by the farmer who occupies the ground it was filled with burnt wood and ashes but he had the curiosity to empty it till he came to the pavement. A wall projects at the further extremity 2 ft. from the end and is about 2 ft. high, this in all likelihood was a kind of cellar under one of the houses.

The farmer shewed me some wrought stones but the inscriptions were so imperfect that I could not pretend to copy them, but I must remark by the way that civility to strangers by no means appears to be a characteristic of the country people of Northumberland more than in Wales. At one cottage I passed this morning close to the Wall, I saw a woman at her door with a sheep dog by her side. As I approached nearer, she shut herself in the house and endeavoured to set the dog on me; had I not been armed with a stick, in all probability I might have been bitten. At the Chesters I have just been speaking of, it was not much better, for the farmer who was in the field with his reapers did not attempt to call off his dog when he was running to me, and it was sometime before I could persuade him that my intentions were pacific in visiting these parts. How absurd is the idea of Arcadian simplicity and benevolence in the lower orders. Whenever *I* have made any observations I am sure it has been quite the reverse, and the more uninformed the people, the more brutal and selfish I have always found them.

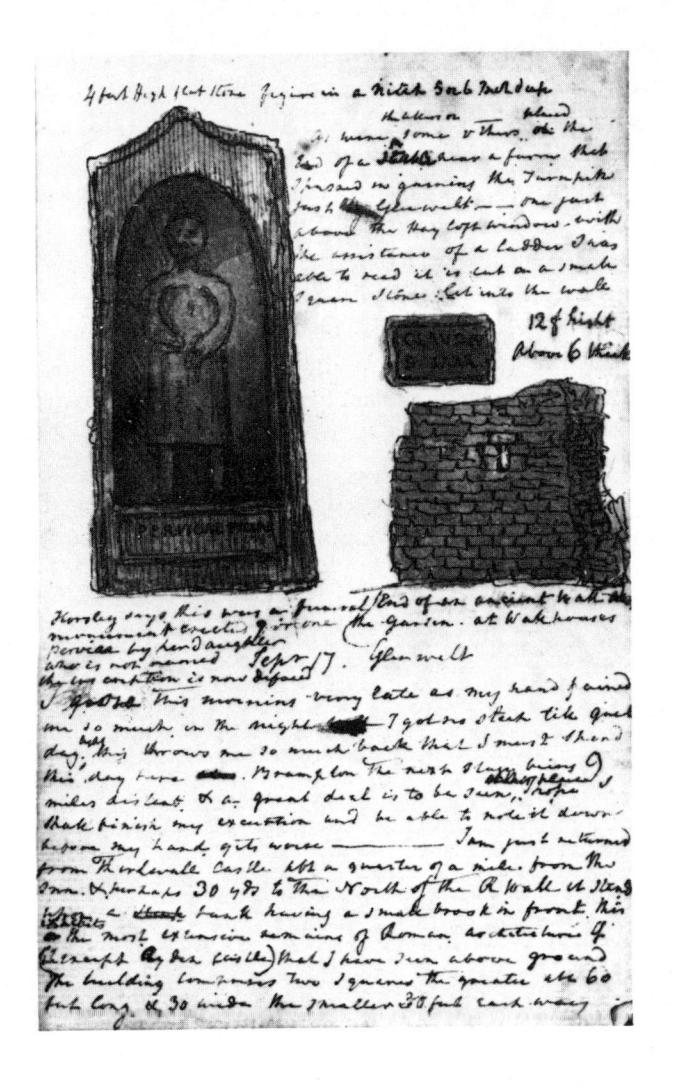

At the mill a little way from the Chesters there were some stones dug up a few months ago and I was very glad I deviated a little to see them. They were found by the miller in soft ground whilst he was clearing a watercourse. The one bearing the inscription on a square stone about 2 ft. long and 1 broad, he has placed on a gateway near his house. The other which is part of a female figure now rests against the wall.

It may be permitted to hazard a conjecture in this place. I should suppose the figure represented the Goddess Victory and stood upon the other stone. How curious is the term Barbarus bestowed on all who were not Roman. In our India regiments we soften the term by calling the officers of our auxiliaries, native cavalry or infantry.

In the Notitia the cohort Sexta Nerviorum is said to have been stationed at Virosidum or Elenborough though no inscription has been found there respecting them. NB. Elenborough is near Maryport on the coast. Horsley supposes that at the decline of the empire this and other cohorts were moved from place to place and that the Sexta Coh. Nerv. which had been stationed in the western part of Yorkshire as appears from an inscription no. 18 of the Brit. Rom. did advance to the station at Elenborough.

About ¾ mile beyond this place I came to a farm called Wallhouse. There are eveident traces of old buildings, and part of a wall 12 ft. high and 6 ft. in thickness is standing. Whether this was the storehouse for corn mentioned in the following inscription on a broken stone close to it one cannot readily determine, but from its situation on fertile ground below the Hill on which the Roman Wall is built, one would suppose it was a very elegible spot for the purpose, and that when those employed by Severus in building the Wall found it had been chosen for the purpose, perhaps by the army under Agricola 130 years before, they rebuilt it from the ground and placed this inscription on the same part of the edifice.

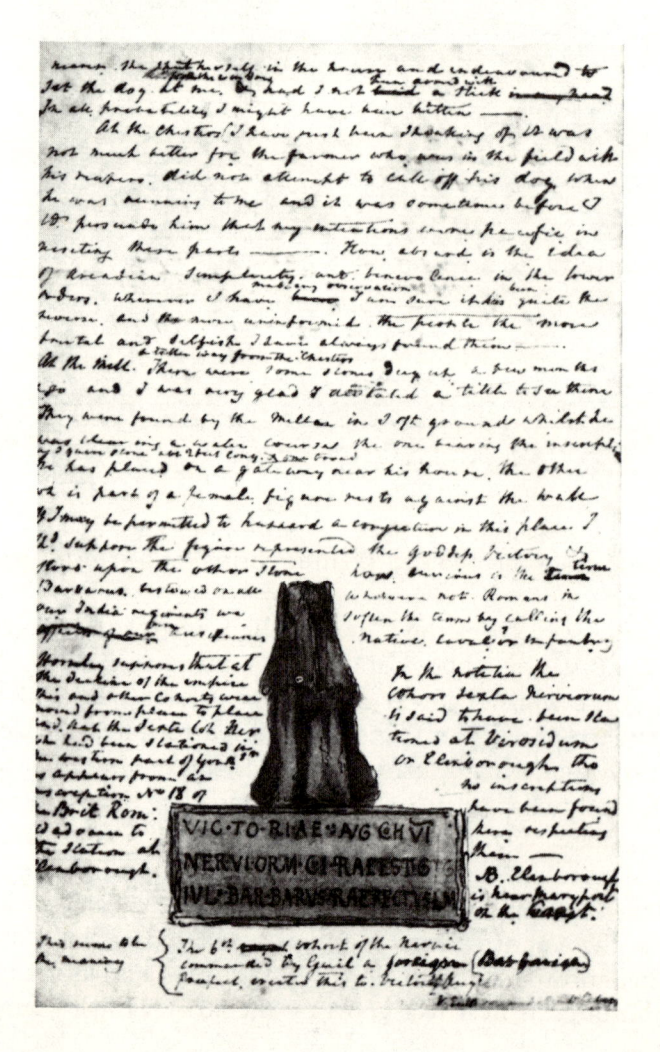

There is another singular stone preserved at the same place but the figure is done in so awkward a manner I should rather imagine it to be British than Roman. There were some characters, an old woman informed me beneath it, but these are defaced by the weather.

September 17th ... GLENWELT
I got up this morning very late as my hand pained me so much in the night I got no sleep till quite daylight. This throws me so much back that I must spend the day here, Brampton the next place being 9 miles distant, and a great deal is to be seen at this place. I hope I shall finish my excursion and be able to note it down before my hand gets worse.

I am just returned from Thirlwall Castle about ¼ mile from the Inn and perhaps 30 yards to the north of the Roman Wall. It stands upon a bank having a small brook in front. This exhibits the most extensive remains of Roman architecture (except Aydon Castle) that I have seen above ground. The building comprises two squares, the greater about 60 ft. long and 30 wide, – the smaller 30 ft. each way. Before I retired to bed my hand became so painful I could scarcely hold a pen.

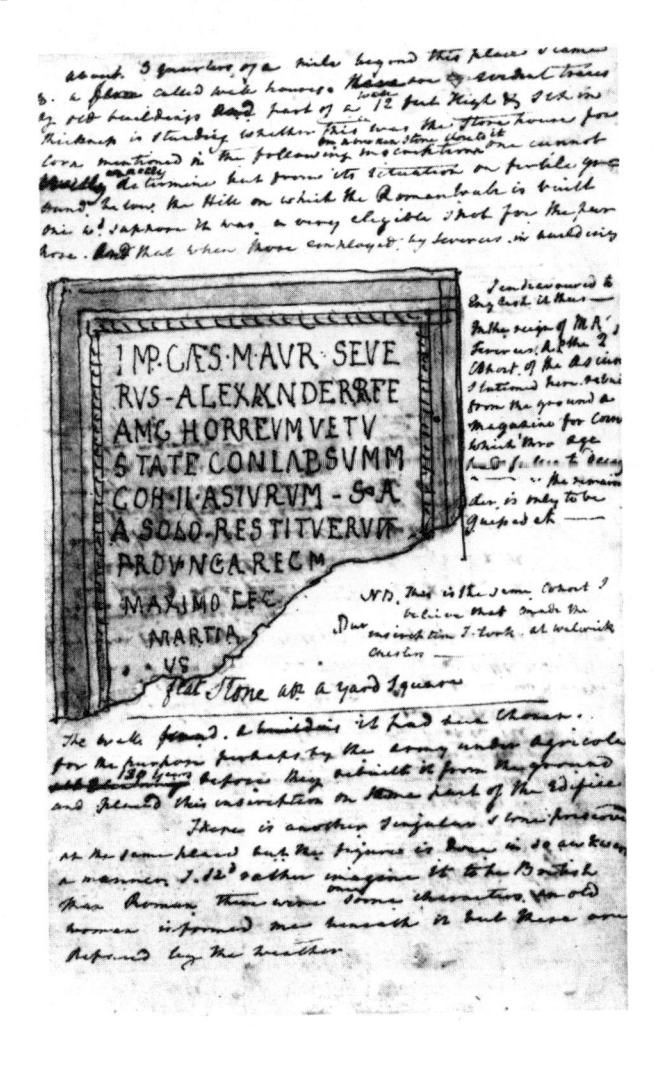

September 18th

I procured no sleep, as the preceding night the inflamation continuing with great violence the whole way up my arm, After breakfast I was persuaded to send to a medical man three miles off to look at it. He came in the middle of the day and lanced it. Towards evening I found it much relieved.

September 19th

My hand was less painful but as I could not use it I found the day very heavy. However I comforted myself as it continued to rain with great violence that had I been well I could not have ventured out.

September 20th

I staid within doors almost the whole of this day; borrowed some books of my landlady, – one a tour through Scotland in 1785 written in a very singular style, and what is worse, conveying but little information.

September 21st
After a good night's sleep I find myself so much refreshed I hope I shall be able to proceed towards Carlisle tomorrow as I must be again in exercise. In the middle of the day I walked round the house and premises and visited Caernorren (or Magna) a Roman station. It is distinctly traced in a grass field of about 4 acres, only a little way from the Inn, and lies between the turnpike and the Roman Wall. The maiden way passed by Blenkinsop Castle, and crossing the brook proceeded to this place; it can only be here and there traced.

September 22nd
At 12 this morning I left Glenwelt and proceeded to trace the Roman Wall from Thirlwall Castle. For the first mile the trench alone is distinct, indeed beyond that little is to be seen of the original structure, 'tho a wall has been built for some distance on the

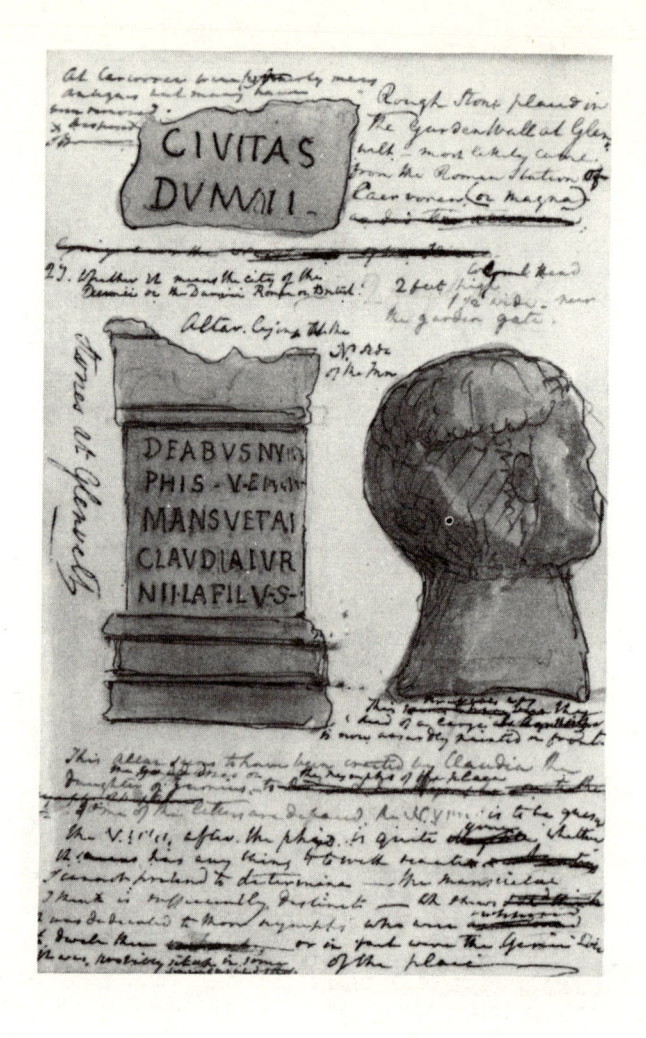

ancient foundation. On making inquiries about ¾ mile beyond Thirlwall respecting some ruins, I observed to the south of this wall, a farmer informed me a few years since there was a building there called the Chapel. This was enclosed by walls of prodigious thickness. On destroying this to build his farmhouse, they discovered underground some wrought stones of a very large size which he blew up with gunpowder in order to employ his work. When giving a description of this place he remarked what the county people have often done before in thinking of the works of the Romans, that they must have been a much larger and stronger race of men than those of the present day. He further added that the quarry was above ½ mile off whence these stones were taken, and that it was reported a line of men from the quarry to the Wall, threw the stones from hand to hand for the service of the masons. How readily do mankind connect the marvellous with ancient occurrences; it has ever been the case and will ever be so till the end of things. Many stones with inscriptions, the farmer said, were purchased at that time by a man who walked about the country as I did, that for his own part his scholarship could never make them out.

After ½ hour walk beyond this place on coming to a high ledge of earth with a brook flowing in a vale beneath, I lost all kind of trace of the Wall and suppose it must have slid away from the bank, – beyond this it is indistinctly traced on the opposite side of the water. Still keeping the higher ground, I then took the direction of the turnpike and got onto it about 4 miles distant from Brampton, and about a mile beyond this I turned down to the right to visit Norwood Castle the ancient seat of the Dacres Barony of Gelersland now belonging to Lord Carlisle. The building is quandrangular having a square tower to the east and west; the approach is through a gateway where I imagine formerly was a drawbridge. The coat of arms and helmet are carved in stone over the arch.

Passing on into the court, one side of which is occupied by Mr. Armstrong the land-steward, I procured a person to attend me to the rooms still furnished and kept up for his Lordship and family who occasionally visit the place. The hall is of large dimensions but dark and uncomfortable on account of its being lit with a number of small windows at the very top. These were probably designed to set off to the best advantage the panels on the ceiling combining painted portraits of all the Kings of England right down from Saxon times. These are said to have been removed from Kirk Oswald Castle when it was destroyed nearly three centuries ago. Certainly the paintings are curious for their antiquity, much expression or diversity is not to be expected.

The fireplace to this large room was in an arch 15 or 16 ft. in span certainly wide enough to roast an ox or an elephant. From hence, passing through two or three antique rooms where the tapestry and furniture appear to be coeval with the external part, I was conducted upstairs into a narrow gallery where are some pieces of armour, from hence into a curious shaped room formerly the library, in a kind of case opening like a fire-screen is a large illuminated Latin manuscript with a long preamble respecting Glastonbury Abbey. If time had permitted I should have much liked to have waded through a page or two; perhaps the monastery at Lancroft close by founded by Robert de Vallibus one of the family, anno 1116, was connected with it. I afterwards passed to another part of the quadrangle through some vaulted passages very strongly guarded to the chapel. This gloomy excavation my conductor informed me had been used as a dungeon by Lord Howard, Warden of the Marches. The chapel, to one fond of genealogies will without doubt afford ample subject for research, as the sides and ends exhibit coats of arms and badges expressive of the marriages and intermarriages of the Dacres and Howard families from generation to generation. From one, I recollected that this domain and others were granted by Henry II to Robert de Vallibus I think it was, or his father. The ceiling of the Chapel has the same kind of portraits as were exhibited in the Hall but they seem much better preserved. Mine was too cursory a view of this ancient edifice, but I was obliged to quit it in order to have time to look at the Priory nearly a mile beyond, before evening closed in. In the way to the Priory which is situated to the north of the river Irthing, I passed two bridges of two arches each, the further one as an inscription on it informed me, was erected in the time of James II at the expense of the County. The two arches of the first bridge are well turned, and the whole structure has a light effect. This, I imagine is more ancient than the other which was probably found necessary in the time of floods.

Lancroft Priory is cruciform, very much the same style of architecture as Brinkburn Abbey. It is built of red sandstone which gives it a singular appearance. The nave is now employed as a parish church and kept in good preservation. The tower and east end chapels are unroofed and falling fast to decay. I have observed some monuments to the Dacres, but had not leisure to decipher the inscriptions. A stone erected some years back to the right of the Communion Table possesses the date of the foundation of the Priory before given. The height of the roof must render it very difficult for the voice of the reader, but any accommodation might destroy the appearance of the building.

I cannot say that the dwelling-houses round the church amongst which was that of the clergyman's, present a much better external than the decayed edifice, but all ideas of comfort as well as of other things are by comparison. It was nearly dark before I was on my road to Brampton $2\frac{1}{2}$ mile distant, but at the end of my stage I happily found my comfortable Inn – The White Lion. N.B. Lancroft Priory is a perpetual curacy increased by Queen Anne's Bounty.

September 24th

After breakfast this morning accompanied by a gentleman who kindly offered to be my conductor, I took a walk about 2 miles south of Brampton to see an inscription made by the Romans on the side of a rock above the river Gelt. It is probable they had a stone quarry there during the time they were building the Roman Wall and that the Agricola here mentioned was not the Roman general but an inferior officer (Optio) under the centurion who had the command of the soldiers employed on the occasion. The inscription is read thus, though I must confess I did not find part of it sufficiently legible to give any significance to the characters- VEX LEG II AUG OB VI APRO E MAXIMO SUB AGRICOLA OPTIO CONSULTIBUS OFICINA MERCATII MERCATIUS FERMI . . . Vexallatio Legionis Secundae ob virtutem Augusta appellata sub Agricola optione Apro et maximo consultibus et officina Mercatii Mercatius filius Fermii.

The stone in this quarry is red of a sandy kind though it is evidently very durable. Some of the views on the little river Gelt are truly romantic. High rocks of red and white stone covered with foliage rise high above the river which is shallow and rapid and very serpentine in its course. The jutting points of the rocks form great variety in the scenery. This stream rises in the moors and is of a dark colour; the trout caught in it are excellent.

Brampton is thought to have been the Brimitenracum of the Romans and is more populated that I should have imagined from its extent, containing above 1600 souls. A little to the north of the town was a Roman station called Petriana. A Mr. Johnson, who owns the Estate, has built a house on the very spot. On clearing the ground, many altars and stones with inscriptions were discovered, and in one part underground a room supposed to have been used as a Bath attracted much attention of the Antiquarian, but this is no longer preserved. Between this and Magna was a very large station called Amboglanna now Bardoswald. I missed seeing this yesterday when I lost trace of the Wall which passed the water just at this spot instead of keeping to the side of it as I imagined. Mr. Horsley has collected no less than 25 different inscriptions from Magna made chiefly by the first cohort of Alia Dacorum quartered here. On looking over Hutchingson's History of Cumberland this morning, I met with a note which threw a good deal of light upon some of the inscriptions I have seen. It mentions that beside the regular Roman troops there were many foreign auxiliaries stationed along the line who took their names either from their country or adopted some in compliment to their commanders, indeed I had imagined this must have been the case from the altar I observed at Housesteads. As very little is to be seen or learnt respecting the Roman Wall between this and Carlisle I believe, I shall take the turnpike instead of crossing through the enclosures which would be almost a Herculean labour to little purpose.

The whole of the way from Brampton to Carlisle is flat and uninteresting, but just on entering the city there is a fine view of the River Eden as far as I could judge by moonlight, for it was above 10 o'clock when I got to the end of my stage.

September 25th . . . CARLISLE

As I wished very much to conclude my observations on the Wall, I proceeded about 11 o'clock this morning on my road to Bowness, 14 miles distance. The day was exceedingly beautiful which could not but render my walk agreeable, although neither the country a dead flat the whole of the way, nor the effect of my search afforded much interest to me. To Kirkandrew, a small village 3 miles distant from Carlisle, not the least traces are to be discovered of the Wall or trench excepting by chance when ploughing the land, – they now and then turn up items belonging to the foundations. At Burgh another little place, I was equally unsuccessful in endeavouring to trace it, though this is supposed to have been another of their larger stations; – one intelligent person I met (schoolmaster-curate of the place) walked with me into a field to the west of the village where he said he would show me the direction it took. I thought I could here perceive a gentle rise in the ground for some way out on entering the field. About 50 yards distant before we came to this spot a trench is very visible; this he informed me might be discovered running in a parallel direction for some distance which naturally leads one to suppose it to be part of Adrian's Vallum.

At a house in the village is possessed a stone with an inscription which I shall endeavour to procure a sight of tomorrow. Beyond Burgh all the way to Drumburg the road runs across some marshes affected by the high tide; not the least can be here found traces of the Wall, nor it can be otherwise conjectured which direction it took than by drawing an imaginary line across the marsh at this point. In such a situation as this I think we may account for the disappearance of the ancient structure without the assistance of farmers and inhabitants of the country. Some part may have sunk into the soft ground or covered by the mud gradually rising above it. Others might have been borne away by the violence of the waters, for in the course of so many centuries, what may not be affected by the storm and changes of so large an estuary as Solway Firth? At Drumburg instead of finding the remains of a Roman Castle as I expected, I was disappointed finding an old mansion formerly belonging to the Dacres(?) but now the property of the Earl of Lonsdale, converted into a farmhouse, though the farmer's wife seemed indeed to think it so much her castle that she was very angry at my looking at the outside and imagined I had no very proper motive for so doing, – from hence it is about 3 miles to Bowness. For the first 2 miles I endeavoured in vain to form a connected line where the Wall ran, though here and there a gentle rise in the fields told me where it had stood. The last mile it is very visible being in some parts nearly 6 ft. high, but this is only the middle of the Wall, the facing stones having long since been taken away, but such is the strength of the cement that this monument of Roman masonry bids fair to remain for ages if it has only the elements to contend with. The middle stones seem to have been more methodically arranged here than in other places, and appear in the section here offered to observation [drawing]* placed in a manner one over the other. This is different from what I have elsewhere remarked, as they seemed first to have made the foundation and facing and then to have thrown in the stones promiscuously. I arrived at Bowness about 5 o'clock and found much better accommodation than I had reason to expect from the outside of the house. I took some [medicine?] as I did not find myself quite "comme il faut", and went to bed before nine o'clock.

September 25th . . . BOWNESS
Rose early this morning and made this circuit of Bowness which still covers a good deal of ground though it was once more extensive. Some of the old houses surrounded by high walls and outer gateways remain evident memorials of the precautions used against the plunderers from the other side of the water even in later times. At the western extremity of the village I could easily trace the line of this Roman station. It was bounded by a trench and might have been about 130 yards each way. Two inscriptions I got sight of; one is now placed over the entrance of a Barn and the characters appear much ruder than I have ever seen; the other is in possession of a person who found it in his garden just on the western extremity of the station which was bounded by a deep trench. The one over the barn door I was obliged to procure a ladder to decipher. It seems to have been inscribed but is now illegible. The other stone is so much mutilated and the inscriptions so very much defaced that it is not possible for so young an antiquarian as myself to guess at it, but some words lead me to imagine that it had been placed as a memorial of some votive offering. The person in whose garden it was found I know not on what authority, supposed it to have been a dedication to Venus, – but as he also supposed the remnant of the first work to have been the termination of JOANNES meaning King John, I cannot say I laid much stress upon his supposition. However he seemed to have had tolerable smattering of Latin, and repeated the whole of the inscription on the Pillar I afterwards viewed near Burgh, I was also indebted to him for a sight of the stone coffin and font represented in the sketch, and an ancient lid of a tomb bearing the arms of the Dacres on which the Dial in the Churchyard now stands. This civility I the more esteemed on account of its variety, for "Les gens de Northumberland sont encore plus rudes envers les etranger que les paysans pays de Galle".

Left Bowness without seeing the Castle sands as I had intended, where in all probability were forts beyond the extremity of the Wall; a mile further to the westward were mounds covered with earth. I was at first surprised that the Romans should have

* Drawing not reproduced—Ed.

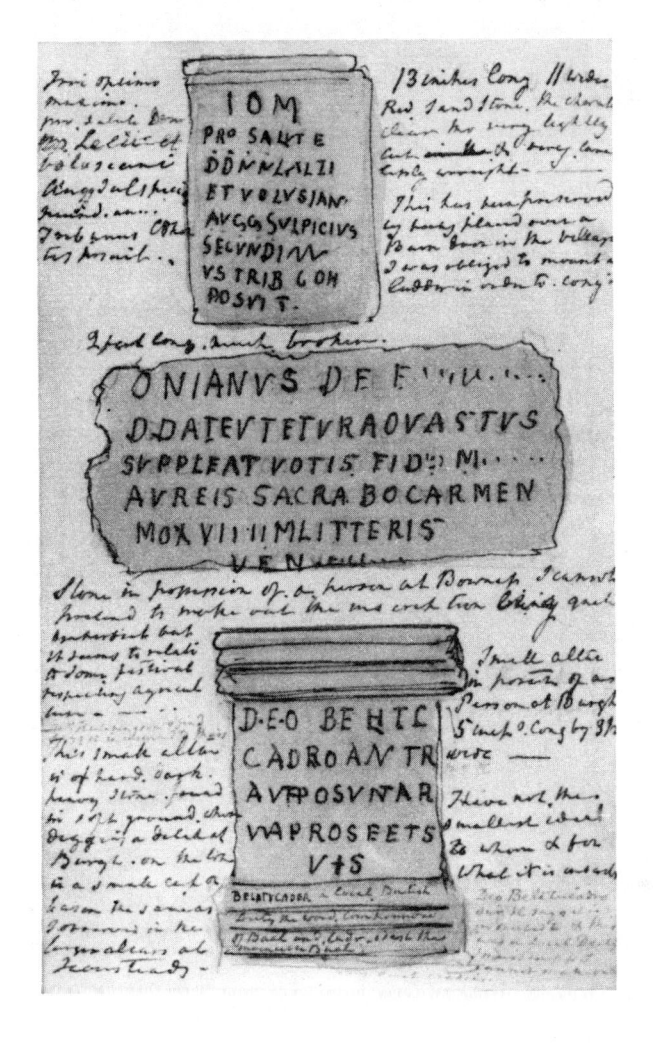

thought it necessary to extend the Wall as far as Bowness since the Firth, almost as high up as Burgh, seems a natural barrier against the incursions of the Northern natives, but I was fully convinced of the necessity for these operations when I saw this estuary at low water when it is fordable in most parts, but dangerous to those unacquainted with the sands. Returning by Drumburgh, I was determined to see whether there were any traces of the Wall on the higher ground to Easton, and accordingly struck up the fields in that direction but to no purpose, and it is still a great doubt with me which course it took; whether over the marsh, or whether it deviated from the direct line to keep the rising ground to the south. On the marsh I observed an embankment thrown up near Drumburgh and others far more extensive nearer Burgh. As Edward I was encamped in this place, we may suppose they were his works. The pillar erected to his memory anno 1645 by the Duke of Norfolk is within a mile of this spot, and apt emblem it is of the nullity of human pride. I hope I do not injure the memory of the said Duke by supposing his object in erecting this column was rather to commemorate his own titles and grandeur than the greatness of the English monarch; but this I suppose was the case, for nearly one whole side was occupied in setting forth who and what *he* was, whereas a few lines were sufficient for the greatest warrior that ever filled the English throne. But behold! how vain are human wishes and endeavours when the more we are designed by nature to be, a few feet of the meanest earth were sufficient to contain this once powerful noble, whose estates and titles extended to the utmost counties of the Kingdom, and the pillar he fondly imagined would carry his name down and that of the monarch through countless ages, is now overturned and scattered in pieces over the plain!

    At Burgh I was sufficiently fortunate to meet with the clergyman I had seen the day before who procured me the sight of a little altar in possession of a Mr. Wilson. It is only 5 in. high and I endeavoured to copy the inscription which I cannot the least comprehend. The stone it is made of is very heavy and has a small basin scooped on the top as in the larger altars. Whether it was a pedestal for some of the household deities, a more skilful antiquary may perhaps determine. Another mutilated stone I was shown dug up at Burgh, inscribed to Hercules and the other deities of the Augustan cohorts. My conductor, the curate of the place had only a salary of £25 per annum besides the Parish School to depend on for himself, wife and five children. Adjoining the little church, he showed me a very strong chamber having iron gates with loopholes to the outside and steps ascending either for observation or the discharge of arrows. This was a place of refuge against the depredations of the Scots, who used frequently to cross the water and carry off the cattle and plunder, and seem to have little respect for things human or divine. Some curious accounts of these predatory excursions are fresh in the minds of some of the inhabitants of the Borders.

It was nearly eight o'clock before I arrived at Carlisle; and I was glad to get my dinner not having eaten anything for twelve hours, and in all must have walked twenty miles. Carlisle Luguvallum Walls and Castle were built about the time of William Rufus though it was a large place in the time of the Romans.

September 26th ... CARLISLE

Wrote some letters after breakfast and walked round the city. I cannot say I was particularly struck with it. The Cathedral is a heavy structure built of red stone; the houses generally speaking are awkward and inconvenient; the outer walls and gate still remain. Within these two years there has been discovered a subterranean passage running a great way and connected to the Castle. As so many accounts have been written respecting this ancient place and collected in Hutchinson's "History of Cumberland" I shall refer to him at my leisure.

About 1 o'clock, I left Carlisle having caused my portmanteau to be forwarded to Keswick, and I contrived to put a change of linen in my knapsack with the rest of my luggage. In time I shall acquire the independence of Diogenes, who threw away his wooden bowl when he found he could drink out of the hollow of his hand. My walk to Wigton was dreary in the extreme, it rained almost the whole of the way an unagreeable accompaniment to a bleak heath over which the road passed. I had been directed to a Public House by the roadside "The Red Dial" eleven miles from Carlisle where I was informed there was good accommodation, but when I came to the house I found the people so uncivil and everything so dirty and uncomfortable that I made the best of my way to Wigton a mile or so to the north. Had I gone direct to the town it would have saved me two miles, but such occasions we must not complain about but take them as we find them. It was about five when I got to the "Queen's Head", Wigton and employed the evening till bedtime in finishing my Journal.

September 27th ... WIGTON

I cannot help noting down some dreams that took such strong possession of my mind last night, I can almost recollect every particular. Were I superstitious and imagine with old Homer, that dreams were from Jupiter I should suppose they betokened a speedy conclusion to my wanderings. In the first place I conceived I was endeavouring to cross an unbounded plain; night suddenly overtook me and so great was the darkness I knew not which way to turn. Methought Pincher (the little terrier I lost last year in Wales) was with me. Fearful of separating from him in the horrid obscurity I called him by his name very frequently and very loud. Suddenly a number of voices in the air in a kind of chorus sounded the name of Pincher. At first they seemed just over my head, gradually dying away to a greater distance. A violent discharge of artillery sounded and the horizon became illuminated for a great way round; again it was dark, and stumbling, I fell into a deep pit and was so much bruised by my fall that I imagined my last moment had arrived. I remember nothing further of this part of the dream, but suddenly the scene changed and I found myself on board a small sloop lying upon a rocky shore dry upon a beach with perpendicular cliffs such as I had observed on passing the Yorkshire coast. The tide came in very rapidly and soon the vessel was afloat. Fearful of being driven on the rocks, I desired a little boy who was my only companion to hoist the sail and endeavour to steer her out to sea. How strongly did I experience in my sleep the sensations of being lifted up as it struck against the rocks at the bottom. Instead of getting out to sea the sloop continued drifting sideways along the shore until a prodigious swell which I observed coming at a distance, at once overwhelmed the barque, and so great was the shock, I awoke.

It is singular that my dissolution should be marked out so distinctly in two such opposite occurrences, but more singular is it that on falling asleep again, I should dream of perishing in a manner that never could stir the imagination of a waking person however it might be in the fairy-tale descriptions or inventions. Methought I was left quite naked in a very lofty chamber at the bottom of a coal pit, and though I had no wings, I had the power of moving from place to place either fanning the air of the ceiling which appeared to be above 100 ft. from the ground, or skirting round the sides of the chamber; but one peculiarity attended my being at the ceiling, I felt as though my head pressed strongly against the top as light bodies do when restrained from rising in water, and it was with great difficulty that I could detach myself. The whole time I was flying about I thought I was singing very loud a song ascribed to General Wolff! but what is more extraordinary, three schoolfellows whom I had not seen for many years, the two Mitfords and Revely seem to be placed in the same situation as myself and occasionally joined in my song. At once, part of the chamber fell in and crushed my companions. I was lost in astonishment at the sight when a fragment fell on me also, it stunned me without killing me and I felt the most excruciating pain in my left side (just in a part I used to blister) and a harsh voice exclaimed "Now I have got you I will gnaw you". Finally a kind of convulsion woke me and happily finished my dreams for the night but as Clarence says it was a long time before I could persuade myself it had been a dream.

With regard to the two first dreams, I think I can trace the main chain of ideas that gave rise to them. My passing over the dreary heath on my way to Wigton was sufficiently impressed on the mind, and my noting down before I went to bed sufficient to render the impression stronger; this formed the groundwork of my first excursion of fancy. The second I can account for in nearly a similar manner, for in reading over last night that part of my Journal relative to the loss of the boat at Shields where six persons were drowned, I had the feeling how nearly I had been in the same predicament having been just before on the spot where the accident happened. For the third concerning the coal-pit, I am indebted entirely to my imagination, for having contrary to my usual custom, eaten a supper which I suppose made me feel oppressed and gave the unpleasant sensation of confinement at the roof of a pit and very probably affected my digestion. I like to endeavour to account for things of this kind, for although Colonel Gardiner's dreams and that of Constantine are recorded by credible persons and have been received by some as preternatural, I must confess I never was of the same opinion on these grounds that if the Deity wished to make any revelations to mankind or communicate anything for their benefit, it might be done in a more decided way than the uncertain channel of dreams.

Left Wigton about one o'clock; it is a place of some size but contains nothing particularly worthy of notice. On returning towards the "Red Dial" (the house I quitted last night) in order to get to the Cockermouth road, I was drawn aside to the left to visit a Roman station very strongly situated on the rising ground, three parts surrounded by a deep dell with a brook running in the bottom. On the banks are quarries of red stone besides the natural trench, a double vallum may be traced almost the whole of the way round the works. It must have been a very strong position by nature, and appears to have also been well fortified by art. Within the inner trench there seems to be all of 12 acres covered with heaps of stone and rubbish. This station was only eleven miles from Bowness and was without doubt a place of great consequence. I have yet to inform myself of particulars concerning the troops stationed here, etc. Most of the stones employed on the Wall at Bowness must have been carried from Wigton as there is no quarry nearer. Striking across a large common, which, by the way seems to be of very fine soil, were it enclosed, I took the direction to Ireby, and mounting the higher ground about three miles further, a most extensive prospect opened to my view. To the north is Solway Firth stretching beyond Bowness with the mainland on the other side; on a clear day Scotland may be seen. To the east, the lower ground has within these few years been enclosed to the amount of about 7,000 acres. In one parish, a clergyman who had the advowson just before enclosure took place, had disposed of his patronage to Lord Lonsdale for £500; unfortunately the tithes came to more than that on annuity, his Lordship having had some dispute with the farmers takes them in kind. To the south-east, Skiddaw and a range of mountains strike along towards Bassenthwaite Lake, and I must confess I felt a gleam of satisfaction sweep across my mind at the first sight of this wild country such as I have not experienced for some years. I shall not at present analyse the subject, but it is certainly true that not all the fertility of the newly enclosed country and the ideas they necessarily excited of progressive improvement, have the same power to please me as the broken line of these barren mountains, that never can be serviceable to mankind.

At Ireby, which is a very small place, I with difficulty procured some eggs, but the civility of my host made amends for all deficiencies and I hope will prove a fortunate beginning to more hospitable treatment than I have experienced for sometime back, but I do not wish to become misanthropic; tourists think highly of the kindness and simplicity of the inhabitants of this country as they do of the Welsh, but alas! I did not experience it, and yet it is not difficult to please me where only the intention is good.

After my repast my host walked nearly half a mile to point out the road to Bassenthwaite where I designed to take up my first station. Stepping aside into a field to the left, he showed me a circular barrow about twenty yards in diameter which within these two years had been dug up for the sake of stones to mend the roads. Under the pile of stones which were heaped up, they came to four fragments of a large chest faced out to form a square of about 7 ft. long and 3 ft. wide; over this was a lid, but nothing was discovered in the inside. Three miles distant on the side of a hill to the north-east two of a similar construction were found not long since. Indeed, he remarked on two or three places on this heath between Carlisle and Wigton where many a severe contest has been fought there are little eminences of this kind, so it is easy to imagine that all along the flat ground bordering on this line the name of Golgotha may be applied to the country almost all the way from Newcastle to Bowness without being a very improper appellation. Arrived at Ouse Bridge at the bottom of Bassenthwaite Lake a little after six o'clock.

September 28th .... BASSENTHWAITE or rather OUSE BRIDGE

As I purpose taking a separate account of my excursions by the Lakes I shall not dwell upon a description of Bassenthwaite in this place. The accommodation seems to be comfortable, and I shall make it my headquarters for two or three days in order to have leisure to view Skiddaw, Caermot [?] and Cockermouth before I proceed to Keswick.

After breakfast, according to the instructions of the landlord, I proceeded due north from the Inn towards Caermot, a hill in a straight line only three miles from Ouse Bridge, but I unfortunately made it nearly twice that distance by mistaking another eminence to the left the object of my search besides wandering in a wood for a considerable time. I crossed a boggy heath, not only very fatiguing and unpleasant but really dangerous in some places. However I learnt one lesson, and that was not to rely too much on my own skill and observations in a country like this where I scorned the idea of a guide and indeed, if I had only taken the right road a little way back I should have had no occasion for one, but often I have been shown this hill at a distance and thought I could not possibly mistake it and supposed accordingly.

Caermot is a range of high ground or what is called in this country a Fell, about a mile long. To the south, it runs into a steep round hill from the top of which is an extensive view of Solway Firth and Scotland, and on a clear day the Isle of Man, Skiddaw and the range of mountains bordering Bassenthwaite Lake are seen to great advantage from this eminence. But what chiefly attracts the traveller to this spot are traces of a Roman Encampment a little way further to the West. A single vallum encompassing an area of about two acres is very distinctly traced, though I did not observe any remains of buildings as at Old Carlisle, which makes me rather suppose it was a summer station or camp. Beyond this, are some cairns or barrows, two of them which are quite at the extremity of the Fell to the north I observed had semi-circular entrenchments carried on the outside, instead of being surrounded by it. I know not whether these works may be attributed to the British or Romans, and near this entrenchment which borders on a quarry where they get limestone, the workmen a short while since discovered some human bones near the surface of the earth, indeed, as I have before observed there is scarcely a hill that does not have some memorial of this kind of expression of the destruction of mankind ... "Homo homini lupus" is an old adage, and both ancient and modern history are nothing but the recital of occurrences that confirm its authenticity.

Returning home in a rather moralising mood that is out of humour both with myself and my fellow creatures, I sat down with a temper disposed to indulge in the most unpleasant ideas, but I am happy to say that by the time that dinner was concluded I was brought to myself again. The uncommon attention of my host and his wife contributed not a little to introduce more favourable sentiments, and I had candour enough to ask this simple question, – "Have I, because I have been unfortunate, the right to entertain unfavourable ideas of others?" Those who appear selfish and hard-hearted to me who am a stranger, have without doubt friends and kindred to share their affection; what have I to expect but disinterested attention from people of this description. Universal philanthropy may appear very good in theory, but am I possessed of it myself? If not, why should I expect it from those whose ideas and observations are much more bounded than my own. Well, to conclude this "much ado about nothing" I will go to bed.

September 29th . . . OUSE BRIDGE

At ten o'clock this morning I set out for Cockermouth five miles distant. In order to have a long day I ordered my dinner here at half-past five and followed the direction of the little river Derwent at the bottom of the Lake as near as I could to Isel, a village about three miles walk from the Inn. The view of the bridge and the church from the

Isel bridge on the river Derwent

bank of the river is very interesting, and a gentleman's house a little beyond embosomed in trees, appears to be an agreeable retirement. In the churchyard at Isel there seems to be two ancient gravestones with all manner of inscriptions, but worn away. On mounting the hill above the bridge a dreary heath continues all the way to Cockermouth and the same misfortune that attended me in my walk to Wigton, for it rained incessantly; however I was determined to persevere, and visited the old castle in spite of the wind and weather.

This is a large, square fortress on an eminence on the south bank of the Derwent. The Gateway, walls and towers are of wrought stone of great thickness. In the interior there are the remains of a large chapel-hall and dwelling apartments, and a vaulted dungeon of considerable height; the arch is supported by a pillar in the centre. This castle is said to have been built just after the Conquest by William de Meschines but it appears to me that the interior was erected at different times, for some of the windows are square, some Gothic, some I had observed in the Castle at Aydon, indeed, these seemed to be a mixture of all kinds of architecture. Part of it is still inhabited, and were a little money expended a great part of the building might be rendered serviceable for a warehouse, etc., etc.

At a stationers at Cockermouth I bought a sketch-book and pencil and fortunately procured a sight of Hutchinson's "History of Cumberland" as I wished to refer to him respecting the Roman station at Old Carlisle. I find that the Ala Augustus Gordiana afterwards styled Herculanus was quartered here; many inscriptions dug from this place have been preserved and inserted in his works. A military way on which the turnpike now runs passed by this station from Ellenborough and took the direction towards the Wall.

Cockermouth seems a pretty considerable town built on the junction of the rivers Derwent and Cocker. I cannot say it is very prepossessing in respect to appearance for I saw it to every possible disadvantage and perhaps might have been rather influenced against it. My return to Ouse Bridge if anything, was worse than my walk from it, for now the rain took me in front and completely drenched me in the course of a few minutes as though I had been swimming in the Derwent, but as the Frenchman observed "C'est la fortune de la guerre" therefore one must make the best of it. About half-past four I arrived at my quarters and was a new figure by dinner-time dressed up in the produce of my host's wardrobe. I should not have noticed this had it not afforded some entertainment to two gentlemen who arrived about 6 o'clock . . . their equipage on the other hand, greatly attracted my attention. They had driven a blind mare all the way from Edinburgh. Their chair-springs were broken, and what was worst of all the poor animal had fallen lame, still they purposed reaching Kendal tomorrow. I found out one is the proprietor of the circus at George's Fields.

September 30th . . . OUSE BRIDGE

It rained very much this morning, but during a cessation for a few minutes I took a sketch of the bridge near the Inn and the appearance of the Lake in front of the house; afterward I rowed for nearly a mile on the water but was obliged to return completely wet through. Coloured my sketches after dinner; read some pages from Seneca; transcribed the substance of what I had read and was not in bed till nearly twelve o'clock.

October 1st . . . COCKERMOUTH

This morning fortunately was more promising. Left my quarters at Ouse Bridge at about 11 very well satisfied indeed with my accommodation there and the reasonableness of the charges. As an instance of my mode of entertainment, one day I had a jack of five pounds weight a chicken, an onion, and afterwards an apple tart for dinner. The charge for eating dinner was 1/6d; tea one penny; the charge for brandy and water, fourpence, etc., etc.

I took the road to Cockermouth for I did not like leaving the curious antique at Bridekirk behind me. My walk I endeavoured to diversify by striking off to a ridge of hills to the right of the turnpike, and the view from hence fully repaid me for the trouble of climbing. In my way through Cockermouth I left the contents of my luggage pockets at the Sun Inn and proceeded immediately to Bridekirk about two miles and a half beyond. Very happy I was in seeing this curious antique (the church font), perhaps the most finished and perfect remains of northern sculpture in the kingdom. Much should I have liked to have had a whole day before me in order to take a more perfect drawing of the font; however, as it was, I took the four sides sufficiently exact to represent the outline of the figures seen.

Returned to dinner at four, and spent the whole evening in reading Hutchinson's History.

October 2nd . . . COCKERMOUTH

It rains almost incessantly. However I must not complain, with a good house over my head and books before me I have sufficient occupation.

Thoughts occasioned by the ruins of the Roman works and the extracts from Seneca.

How are the mighty perished; the silent hand of time has not only swept away generation after generation of this proud and powerful people. These are the people who deemed their fame immortal, but even their works and memorials, which were to transmit their names to posterity and proclaim them the conquerors of the world, now can scarcely be traced. Here and there we meet with fulsome inscriptions to the memory of their officers of their Emperors on altars directed to unknown Gods. The country I have just walked over once echoed with the hurry of busy men, and streets once were thronged with multitudes rushing to the destruction of their fellow creatures or exulting in their victories, now are a heap of rubbish overgrown with weeds. How vain were the efforts of the inhabitants; they fancied themselves secure in their fortifications, superior to the barbarian tribes they had to contend with, – nothing could alarm them. But Death has swept them away; time has continued the work of desolation and scarcely left enough to say "This once was Roman". What am I then, who now contemplate the wreck of ages? . . . an insect, a breath of wind will sweep me away as it has millions before me.

And what is Death that I should shrink at its approach? If it cannot be avoided that is in itself a sufficient reason for one to meet it with firmness. "Cowards die many times before their deaths, the valiant never meet with death but once". The earth itself is in continual change. How many islands are swallowed up in the sea? How many towns do we sail over? Nay, how many regions have been wholly lost either by inundations or earthquakes? Why then should Death strike us with terror? As children are frightened by a vision, so are we terrified by the phantom of imagination. Take away the instruments of death, the fire, the axe, the guards the executioner, the whip and the rack; take away the pomp and the circumstances that accompany it, and death is no more than what I have often experienced in my sickness, nay, even in my dreams. The pain is nothing to a fit of the stone, if it be tolerable it is not great. If it be intolerable, it cannot last long.

There is nothing eternal nor many things lasting, but by divers ways everything comes to an end. What an arrogance is it then when this world itself stands condemned to dissolution that man alone should expect to live for ever? When we should die we will not; when we would not, we must. [Ed. We have omitted a further 12 pages of closely written sermonising.]